Ask the Coach

Practical Solutions to Everyday Challenges in Business and Life

TAMMY HOLYFIELD

WESTBOW
PRESS
A DIVISION OF THOMAS NELSON
& ZONDERVAN

WestBow Press books may be ordered through booksellers or by contacting:
WestBow Press
A Division of Thomas Nelson & Zondervan
1663 Liberty Drive
Bloomington, IN 47403
www.westbowpress.com
1 (866) 928-1240

ISBN: 978-1-4908-3906-6 (sc)
ISBN: 978-1-4908-3907-3 (hc)
ISBN: 978-1-4908-3905-9 (e)
Library of Congress Control Number: 2014909874

Printed in the United States of America.
WestBow Press rev. date: 06/12/2014

Contents

About the Author

TAMMY HOLYFIELD, Leadership Expert, Author and Speaker.

Tammy Holyfield is a dynamic speaker, leadership expert, and best selling author, on a mission to teach and inspire people to improve their everyday life. Using the methods and principles she teaches, Tammy has overcome great obstacles, failure, poverty and abuse. Her message and empowering communication style has helped so many find hope and restoration.

Holyfield began her professional career in marketing and served as the Director of Marketing for Summit Pet Product Distributors, the IAMs Pet Food (Proctor and Gamble) regional distribution center.

Tammy is the founder and CEO of Holyfield Consulting, a personal and business development company. Holyfield Consulting specializes in organizational development, strategic planning, communication, building trust, strengthening teams, leadership development, increasing accountability and executing results.

As part of her passion to help others succeed, she shares wisdom and insight in the radio program and column entitled "Ask the Coach"®. Ask the Coach provides a fresh perspective on current challenges facing the business world. Tammy also addresses thousands of people each year from diverse Fortune 500 companies and has consulted and trained entrepreneurs, CEO's, professionals and individuals from all walks of life. Her ideas are proven, practical and get results. And clients say that working with Tammy created an increase in moral, solidified corporate culture, and bridged the communication gap from vision to results. Her audiences and clients agree, Tammy teaches techniques and strategies that are easy to understand and put to use immediately to achieve greater results in their lives and careers.

Her work has been on Amazon's Best Seller list, she co-authored with the legendary business development expert, best-selling author and speaker, Brian Tracy. "Counter-Attack: Business Strategies for Explosive Growth in the New Economy" features Brian Tracy along with leading experts from around the world across diverse fields of business.

We would love to hear from you. Please connect with us on Social Media or visit our website.

Facebook – TammyHolyfield

LinkedIn – http://www.linkedin.com/in/tammyholyfield

Twitter – http://twitter.com/TammyHolyfield

www.TammyHolyfield.com

Dedication

I dedicate this book to my son Chase

Dear Chase,

Thank you for your unwavering faith in the plan of God for our lives. I cherish every year we have worked together whether in full time ministry, speaking events or producing the radio show. You have given faithfully countless hours and always with a genuine servant's heart. You are my inspiration and my motivation. I thank you for waiting with patient expectation to see the fulfillment of God's promises. You are more than an overcomer and I am so grateful for you.

All my Love,
~ Mom

Thank you, God for loving me so much that you sent your only Son, Jesus to save me. Thank you for showing me who you are, so I could truly know who I am in Christ.

A very SPECIAL Thank You to ALL the people in my life that never gave up HOPE! Thank you to many great Leaders, Mentors, Pastors and Teachers that helped shape the principles and strategies shared in these stories.

Thank you, Amy Lucas for seeing and staying true to the vision. Even in the wilderness, you stepped out of your comfort zone and trusted God to keep His promise. I appreciate your dedication and hard-working lifestyle. I am continually impressed by your drive and tenacity to not only learn but master new skills, new business models and personal challenges. You are a blessing and I am grateful for you.

Thank you, Tim Ricafrente for not giving up, for embracing the unknown, and for continually challenging me to prove my cause. I also appreciate your help with the research and editing of this project. I know it has not been an easy road, but I know God always sends people to help you grow and to develop areas of your life in preparation for His future plan. I know that God sent you and I am grateful for every difficulty and challenge that we have had to endure and overcome.

Author Photo on Cover – Photo Credit: Ashleigh G. Crawley

Introduction

There are countless times throughout our daily interactions both business and personal when we feel weary or burdened by the continuous press of issues and challenges. It's at those moments of fatigue and weakness that maybe all we need is a little encouragement, someone to listen or a fresh idea to cheer us on and strengthen us to finish our race. That is the role of a "Coach".

As I reflect on the junctures of my own path, there's a consistent element that infused my ability to overcome, to press on to the mark, to endure the present hardship that ages our souls, that element is encouragement. I can remember on every seemingly hopeless occasion when I was poised to quit… the thought that I cannot bare another moment or live through another disappointment, at the very second of despair, I would receive a positive word of inspiration, just enough to fuel the possibility that I'm so close… and I am too far to turn back now. My prayer is that you find HOPE for the journey you are on in the pages of this book.

Though a righteous man falls seven times, he
rises again. – Proverbs 24:16 NIV

Bouncing Back from Failure and Disappointment

Dear Coach,
I have experienced many setbacks, disappointments and failures. I get so excited that it could final happen and then nothing. There are days when I have no hope and often times I feel like giving up on my dream. How can I move forward? –Ready to Live the Dream

Dear Ready to Live the Dream,
Despite our best efforts at some point in life we all experience disappointments, setbacks and failure. It could be a result of a mistake we made or something completely out of our control. The bottom line is that IF you are ever going to try to achieve anything then these circumstances are an inevitable part of life. The major difference between people who succeed and those who don't are their perception and responds to failure.

#1 Be Encouraged... You are in Great Company!
The greatest of achiever have bounced back from failure and disappointment. Challenging your perspective on failure will help you persevere. Every great success story has a failure chapter.

Famous People Who Failed...
Steve Jobs
Michael Jordan
Oprah Winfrey
Henry Ford
Bill Gates
Harland Sanders
Walt Disney
Albert Einstein
Isaac Newton
Thomas Edison
Steven King
J.K. Rowling
Wolfgang Amadeus Mozart... just to name a few!

Helen Keller: Lost her sight and hearing due to a mysterious fever when she was only 18 months old. She overcame her deafness and blindness to become a strong, educated woman who spoke about, and promoted, women's rights.

Winston Churchill: Overcame a stuttering problem and poor performance in school to become Prime Minister of the United Kingdom and one of the most influential political leaders of the twentieth century. He was also known for his powerful and rousing speeches.

#2 Should Have, Would Have, Could Have... Get Rid of Regret!
When we fail we may feel like we have wasted our time but regret lies in not doing. Mistakes are not permanent markers on our egos. The only waste of time is the time spent living with REGRET!

#3 What Can I Learn?
Failure, setbacks and disappointments can actually open your eyes to options you never considered before. Don't be afraid of new and creative ways of solving issues.

#4 Remove the "U" from Failure! It's NOT Spelled Fail U R.

Keep Your Confidence in Yourself. Don't identify yourself with the result or outcome. You are NOT a failure you just tried something that did not work.

#5 Say "Good-Bye" to Yesterday! Let it Go–Forgive.

Holding on to the past will hinder your forward movement. The weight of unforgiveness especially forgiving yourself, can be heavy and not to mention expensive to your health!

Nearly everyone at some point in life has been hurt by the actions or words of another. Holding on to unresolved offenses, hurt or anger is like buried toxic waste waiting to resurface. We can pretend it doesn't exist but over time the harmful effects will seep up and create a mess in our environment. This repressed pain can manifest itself into depression and anxiety; causing bitterness and stealing our joy, peace and victory.

Researchers have recently become interested in studying the effects of being unforgiving vs. being forgiving. Evidence is mounting that holding grudges and bitterness results in long-term health problems. Forgiveness, on the other hand, offers numerous benefits, including: lower blood pressure, reduction in chronic pain and less stress. When you don't practice forgiveness, you may be the one who pays the most.

When you choose to forgive you are not agreeing with the wrong done but more so forgiveness is the act of untying yourself from thoughts and feelings that bind you and delay your victory.

#6 Dream Again.

There is creative power when you allow yourself space and permission to DREAM. Think about the outcomes you want to see. Focus on where you want to be instead of where you currently are when you do you will see a clearer pathway as to how to get there. Don't let the fear or worry of future failure stop you from setting goals and dreaming of the life you want to live! Dream Big!

From the Coach:

Faith is like a SUPERPOWER, that's why someone is always trying to steal it!

Ask Yourself:

What do I REALLY want?

Is what I want and what God wants for my life in alignment?

What I am willing to do to achieve the desired results? Why have I not done it yet?

Seek the Kingdom of God above all else and live righteously, and He will give you everything you need. — Matthew 6:33 NLT

Priority Power

Dear Coach,
It seems as if time is moving faster. I have more "To-Do" on my list than hours in the day. How can I get a grasp on my time?
—Running Out of Time

Dear Running Out of Time,
It does seem as though time has increased its speed. Our weeks seem like a day, we blink and it is gone. We look at the calendar and wonder where the year went. The encouraging report is there are some specific rules that apply to time. Our awareness of these principles is a key indicator as to how we decide to spend what we have. Time is a valuable asset that is perishable. This means that it cannot be saved. We must spend what we have everyday.

We have all heard someone say, "I will take a vacation, get more organized, clean the garage, visit my family, or read more when I get the time." All of us have a "Someday I will list" and we say "Oh, I will get to that when I get more time." The reality is we cannot get more time. This is one area where everyone in the world is equal. We all have the same amount and we have all the time there is. We cannot make it, nor can we save it to spend later. Time, it just keeps ticking and we must spend all of it everyday. There are tremendous amounts of resources on the subject of time management. But I

5

believe we cannot manage time itself. The only thing we can manage is ourselves within the time.

All things require time. No matter what you want to do in life, whether it's work, a round of golf or sleeping that extra few minutes, it requires time. Time is indispensable. Many years ago, I learned a valuable self management and planning rule taught by Brian Tracy. It's called the 10/90 Rule. This rule says that the 10% of time you spend to plan your activities in advance will save you 90% of the effort involved in achieving your desired results. When we take the time to plan it helps us to think through the actions and steps involved in completing the task.

We have also heard people say, "I don't have time for this." What they are really saying is "this" is not important to me. In order to get control of our time we must know our highest priorities. Only then are we able to say "yes" to our goals and "no" to the things that are not in line with what we are trying to achieve.

Time is irreplaceable. Nothing else will do, especially in relationships. Highly successful people understand that time is the only currency that builds relationships at work and at home. Most people equate the amount of time you spend with them to measure how much you care about them.

When I think of time, I think of it as currency in exchange for something else. Our time should be spent in exchange to what really matters to us. We have 168 hours in a week. Evaluating how you are currently spending that time will help in taking control. The average person spends 49 hours per week sleeping, 6.5 hours eating and 40 plus hours working. So that leaves 72.5 hours per week for other activities. When we stop and evaluate we often discover that what we say is important and what we do with our time is different. By planning and making these necessary adjustments, we can gain a greater level of control while living a purposeful and peace life.

From the Coach:

Pray, Plan, Proceed... How do you spend the FIRST hour of your day? Meeting with GOD before meeting with people will produce SUCCESS!

How we spend our time and money are reflections of our true core values.

Ask Yourself:

What are the TOP 10 most important things in my life?

Do my priorities and my calendar reflect how I truly want to live?

How am I spending my time this week?

It was My hand that laid the foundations of the earth, My right hand that spread out the heavens above. When I call out the stars, they all appear in order." Isaiah 48:13 NLT

Clear the Clutter–Getting Your HOME in Order!

Dear Coach,
Every year, my family and I want to start the year right by cleaning up the clutter that we have taking over our lives, but getting started is a big challenge. What should we do to get started?
–Too Much Stuff

Dear Too Much Stuff,
Usually it is when we get to the point of saying, "I have had enough." Is when we get serious about change!

"The secret to being organized isn't about neat and tidy, it's about knowing where to find what you are looking for." –Albert Einstein

When your surroundings are cluttered and disorganized, your life and frame of mind are likely to follow. But when your house is in proper order things seem to go more smoothly at home and in other areas. The truth is we all have a threshold for pain or a level of tolerance for things being out of order. Usually, it is when things get beyond that point that we get serious about making changes. Here are a few tips for making positive orderly changes for any time of the year.

.#1 A place for EVERYTHING and EVERYTHING in its place!
The reason things pile up on counters, tables and floors is because it does not have a "Home". Think about how often and where you use the item and find a place that will work best. For example if you use the item frequently then make it easy and convenient to access but if the item is used only once or twice a year then you can store it in a higher or less convenient location.

#2 Get Rid of it!
I like to PILE and PURGE! Letting go of the personal and emotional attachment to STUFF will help increase order in your life! It's amazing the things we think we can't do without. Start by asking yourself what is really vital to your day-to-day life. Limit the number... do you really need that many? We live in a society obsessed with MORE. The more dishes, laundry and STUFF you have, the more time and energy it takes to manage.

#3 Don't buy storage bins and containers... UNTIL after you have sorted!
Getting organized should not start out as a shopping trip. Often people get a great feeling of BEING organized just by BUYING a storage bin. But that is a false sense of accomplishment. The reality... Wait until after the sorting is done. This is a better option because you are clearer about what you really need.

#4 Organize and Store things AS YOU GO!
Winter, Spring, Summer and Fall all come one day at a time. Try organizing, sorting and storing by the seasons as you go through your day-to-day instead of trying to do the whole house at one time. Although, throwing it in a drawer, closet or box without sorting DOES NOT count!

OR for really outrageously **FAST RESULTS**...
#5 Invite someone you REALLY admire over for dinner. Often we can use events to motivate action. Events give us deadlines and

deadlines can be used as "Forcing Agents." We always get done what we would be humiliated by not doing.

Facts:
Medical studies prove by simplifying your life you will decrease stress and its harmful effects while increasing your memory functions.

Princeton University Neuroscience Institute reports that physical clutter in your environment negatively affects your ability to focus and process information. Clutter competes for your attention. The research also reports that when you un-clutter and organized your environment you will be less irritable, more productive, and better able to process solutions. (Resource: Princeton University Journal of Neuroscience January 2011 Edition)

A few tips for Get in ORDER at WORK
#1 The condition of your desk speaks LOUD! Want productivity to SOAR? Clear everything but the essentials OFF the top of your desk. Create a HABIT of organizing your work space before you leave each day. This will decrease the overwhelming of the morning rush.

#2 Stuffing everything into a desk drawer does not COUNT as being organized. Clean and organize each area of your work environment even the desk drawers and closets. It is important to keep only what is needed. And try putting things back in its place when you are done using it.

#3 Make it PERSONAL while Keeping it in Order… your work space should inspire you.

#4 Filing systems should be simple and easy to manage and include clear labels.

#5 Using technologies can greatly reduce confusion, clutter and the stress of information, paper, photos, books and more.

From the Coach:

Events like having guest over for dinner can give us deadlines and deadlines can be used as "Forcing Agents." Forcing us to clean up the clutter! We always get done what we would be humiliated by not doing.

Ask Yourself:

What room can I organize this week?

Who can help me?

Why is this important to me?

*He reached down from heaven and rescued me; He drew
me out of the deep waters. – Psalm 18:16 NLT*

Overcoming EMAIL Overwhelm!

Dear Coach,
I am drowning in a sea of forever emails. It is hard to focus on getting things done because I am always checking and dealing with someone else's fire or junk offers. Honestly, I am afraid if I don't read them all that I will miss something important. – Need an Email Lifeline

Dear Need a Email Lifeline,
We live in a society where other people think that we must immediately respond to their urgent situations. Recently, I had 12,355 UNread messages so I know what you are saying is true for many of us. According to the Radicati Group estimated worldwide E-mail traffic messages per day: 2012 419 billion.

Email... It's still how we communicate. But does your inbox consume your day? Maybe you feel overwhelmed by the constant checking and rechecking as well as responding and deleting. Here are 5 Practical Tips to Win the Battle!

Schedule

SET boundaries!!! Instead of constantly checking your inbox or smart phone notifications every few minutes schedule time to check and respond to emails. This will reduce interruptions and increase focused productivity.

Sort

There are several online email organizing software solutions, these solutions can automatically sort your emails into categories like "Business" or "Shopping."

Trash

Delete ruthlessly! If it's worth keeping then copy and save it on your computer, print it or create email folders. Here's a great way to look at it... If it were paper would you keep it on your desk?

Unsubscribe

That information may have been useful at one time but do I still need it??? Often times we don't unsubscribe because we don't take the time to go through the process. There are some really cool online solutions to optimize your time.

Outsource

This is a great option for busy people who really need to respond to emails with human interaction. Hire a Virtual Assistant.

Tammy Holyfield

From the Coach:

Usually we feel overwhelmed when we don't have control over a circumstance or situation or when we expect too much from ourselves or others.

Ask Yourself:

What's my email responds standard?

How can I communicate my standard to others?

What can I automate in regards to email?

"So whatever you wish that others would do to you, do also to them, for this is the LAW and the Prophets. – Matthew 7:12 (ESV)

Strategic Leadership

Dear Coach,
Our company is in a state of mass confusion about the future. The rumors are creating fuel for the fire. Our management team needs help to get things back on track and increase production.
–Upside Down

Dear Upside Down,
Change and uncertainty often fosters an environment of fear which leads to a lack of trust. The lack of trust can slow things down and create higher cost of doing business. Building trust and restoring confidence can significantly impact bottom line results as well as employee morale. A more strategic approach to leadership can help your management team turn it around.

Strategic Leadership is the art and science of formulating, implementing, and evaluating decisions that will enable an organization to achieve its desired results. Strategic leaders narrow the focus to four key results areas.

1. **Exceptional Performance**
2. **Loyal Customers**
3. **Engaged Employees**
4. **Unique Contribution**

Exceptional Performance
In the book Good to Great, Jim Collins defines this as sustained superior performance. In the "For Profit" arena that would be top line, bottom line and stock price. In education it may mean graduation rates or test scores. In the "not for profit" arena it may translate to serving the target population to the best of our ability. What defines exceptional performance for your organization? Defining and clearly communicating will help to build trust and confidence.

Loyal Customers
Loyal, not just satisfied customers. Do you have customers who are marketing for you, and referring others? If not, ask why not.

Engaged Employees
Engaged employees are those who use their talents, bring their best to work, know the strategic alignment and who find purpose in their role. They are essential to sustained superior performance. Are your employees engaged in the results of the overall organization?

Unique Contribution
If your organization suddenly went away, would it be missed by the community or society at large? What is your organizations unique contribution?

In addition, leadership style will greatly influence the four key result areas. What is your leadership style? Operational or Strategic?

Operational	Strategic
Make every decision	Develop people to make their own decisions and manage themselves
Tell people what to do	Communicate and unleash talent toward highest priorities
Tell people how to do it	Create aligned systems

Control the systems	Disciplined focus and execution system
Puts out fires	Empowers others
Carrot and stick rewards system	Rewards aligned with organizational values, vision, mission and strategic plans

By utilizing a strategic approach to leadership you can bridge the gap during organizational transition.

From the Coach:

Everyone leads someone. Leadership is influence. You can apply the strategic leadership principles to life at home and work by challenging your thinking and engaging the people entrusted to your direction.

Ask Yourself:

Who do I influence at home and at work?

What kind of Leader would I like to follow?

What can I do to become the kind of leader I would like to follow?

Let us not become weary in doing good, for at the proper time we will reap a harvest if we do not give up. - Galatians 6:9

How to Develop Better Habits

Dear Coach,
I've been trying to complete my goals for years. I think the problem is that I have horrible habits. I try to commit to doing better but I just don't follow through. I need help. –Trying to Reach the Goal

Dear Trying to Reach the Goal,

We are what we repeatedly do. –Aristotle

Habits are routines of behavior that are repeated and tend to occur subconsciously or instinctive. Old habits are hard to break and new habits are hard to form because the behavioral patterns we repeat are imprinted in our neural pathways.

Have you ever heard the saying, "We are creatures of habit."? It's true. It is our nature. A resistance to change is a nature defense. It's our human way of risk management. You can be motivated to change and emotionally resist at the same time. According to our poll here are the top 10 worst habits... although we all have our own list.

Top 10 Worst Habits
1. Gossip
2. Over Spending
3. Poor Time Management

4. Over Eating or Eating Unhealthy Foods
5. Excessive TV, Internet, Social Media or Games
6. Smoking
7. Drinking
8. Cursing
9. Nail Biting
10. Negative Thinking

"Any hope of sustained change begins with discovery."

Why We Form Bad Habits

If you think about it, habits are relatively simple to develop. Look at all the habits you don't like. Now let me ask you, did you have to work hard at developing the habit of overeating or watching too much TV, checking Facebook, Twitter or other social media outlets, sleeping too much, or smoking? Of course not. You just did it long enough, through repetition, until it became a habit. Why did you keep doing it though?

If you examine your undesirable habits closely, you will find that they all have something in common. They all give you some type of feeling that is rewarding to you. Why do people spend hours watching mindless television? Why do people smoke? They do it because it gives them a certain feeling, in some cases, relaxation, stress reduction, or even excitement.

You see, we're not addicted to the actual activity. What we're addicted to is the feeling that activity gives us. Just think of any habit you have that you find undesirable. What positive feelings does it give you? Know that you're getting a "reward" for those bad habits, that's why you continue doing it. We don't do things habitually that makes us feel bad, at least not at the moment that we're engaged in doing it.

The 5 Steps to Developing Habits
1. Begin with Discovery... We suggest a "Habit Inventory"
2. Define the feeling associated with the Habit
3. Develop strong enough reasons why you want to replace the bad with good habits.
4. Educate yourself. Know what it really takes to form or change the habit.
5. Repeat until it becomes a Habit... I read this and thought it was great... Continue on the stairs until you reach the escalator. In other words work at it until it becomes natural.

From the Coach:

Only thinking about today will steal your future. Successful people delay gratification while working on the life of their dreams.

Ask Yourself:

Is what I am doing consistently today, my actions and activities producing the future I want?

What are the things I need to stop doing?

What are the things I need to begin? Or continue?

Procrastination in Progress

Dear Coach,
I am frustrated with procrastination within our organization. With current economical conditions now more than ever we need to get things done efficiently. How can we stop the procrastination? –Working Hard with the Hardly Working

Dear Working Hard,
National studies suggest that roughly 15 to 20% of people are procrastinators. Procrastination is usually not a matter of time management. It is a complex issue dealing with personality, circumstances and motivation. There are millions of reasons why people put things off until later. Most of those reasons can be boiled down to a few root causes. They are fear, lack of desire and skill weakness.

Fear
Fear is one of the root causes of procrastination. Fear can take on many forms. A person may have a fear of failure or fear other people's opinion of the results, so they rationalize why they should wait to complete a task. William James said, "Procrastination is attitude's natural assassin. There's nothing so fatiguing as an uncompleted task." Procrastination takes tremendous energy and mental strength. When we put off doing what we know we should be doing we are

constantly reminded it's not done. Some people even put off making decisions in fear of making the wrong one.

Lack of Desire

When someone places one task over another they are essentially saying this is what is important to me. We spend our time based on our values. There are 168 hours in a week how we spend that time defines our priorities. It is human nature to work towards pleasure and away from pain. Whenever the pain of not getting something done gets to an unbearable point that is went we make the most effort to complete the task. If we lack the desire to complete a task or project then we are easily distracted.

> **"Things that matter most should never be at**
> **the mercy of things that matter least."**
> **−Goethe**

Skill Weakness

If your company's mission is to climb a tree, which would you rather do: Hire a squirrel or train a horse? Sometimes people are just not capable of getting the job done or they have not been properly trained.

Often the cure for procrastination is in looking at the task or project differently. Most people don't think through to the consequences of putting off things until later. Ask what would be the outcome is I don't get this done? Vs. What would be the benefit if it is complete? When you complete a task it gives you energy and momentum to do more. But, if you don't the list of things to do seems to grow and be overwhelming.

Here are a few strategies from recovering procrastinators:

- Break down larger projects into small manageable actions.
- Research shows that evenly spaced regular deadlines work better.
- Determine the pain or consequences of procrastination.

- Find a planning and organizing system that works for you.
- Take a class or attend a seminar to sharpen your skills.
- Change your location or scenery.
- Embrace imperfection. Strive for excellence instead there is a difference.
- Hire out nonessentials. This will allow you to focus on what really matters.
- Schedule down time to recharge and renew.

From the Coach:

Most people have the will to win; few have the will to prepare to win.

Ask Yourself:

What am I putting off until later that I can do now?

What are the consequences of not getting it done? For me? Or for others around me?

What are the benefits of finishing?

Proverbs 10:4 (NIV)
Lazy hands make for poverty, but diligent hands bring wealth.

Build Your Organization by Building Your People!

Dear Coach,
We are experiencing a lack of motivation in our organization. How can we do a better job attracting, motivating and keeping the right people? –Frustrated by Lazy People

Dear Frustrated,
Many organizational leaders are puzzled by unsuccessful attempts to improve morale and retention. Often employees are disengaged due to a lack of clear purpose, direction and accountability. To maximize motivation we need to first communicate clearly expectations and then reward according to results. Here are a few ways to increase motivation in your environment and become a people builder.

Show Appreciation… Every time you say "Thank You." to another person you literally contribute to the increase their self-esteem and improve their self-image. You give them a surge of energy and make them feel that their effort was valuable and worthwhile. You empower and motivate them to do more. This attitude of appreciation will also attract and retain key employees. You will be amazed by how eager other people will be to help you in whatever project you are working on.

Approval and Praise... Psychological test reveal that when children are encouraged, approved and praise by authority figures or people they look up to, their energy levels rise, their heart and respiration rates increase. They are happier and consistently have a positive world view. The same applies to adults when given positive feedback on job or project performance. When you go around praising and giving genuine approval to people for their accomplishments, great and small, you will be surprised by the increased willingness to get more done. Praise and approval produces a healthier environment in the workplace.

Make Others Feel Important... One of the most valuable lessons in leadership today is to make other people feel important. Dale Carnegie was an early proponent of what is now called responsibility assumption. One of the core ideas in his books is that it is possible to change other people's behavior by changing one's reaction to them. Carnegie says, "You can make more friends in two months by becoming interested in other people than you can in two years by trying to get other people interested in you." Making people feel important is like turning on a productivity switch that has been surged with a bolt of lightning. People will work at new levels when they have been made feel like a valuable asset to the overall organization.

Pay Attention When They Talk... Another way to empower others, to build their self-esteem and make them feel important is simply to pay close attention to them when they talk. The great majority of people are so busy trying to be heard that they become impatient when others are talking. Remember, the most important single activity that takes place over time is listening intently to the other person when he or she is talking and expressing him or herself. Listening is an art and a learned skill that makes people feel special and respected.

Take Every Opportunity to Be a People Builder... The most successful leaders and organizations understand the secret to success is being a people builder. Again, the general rules for empowering the people around you, which applies to everyone you meet, are appreciation, approval, and attention. Voice your thanks and gratitude to others. Praise them for accomplishments. And pay close attention to them when they talk and want to interact with you. These three behaviors alone will take motivation to new levels and make you a master of human interaction.

From the Coach:

Keep in mind that most people are not inherently lazy. Inactivity is a result of confusion, fear and lack of self esteem. You can be the encouragement someone needs to reach their full potential and God given destiny. People will often rise to the level of expectation place upon them. Believe the BEST in every person.

Ask Yourself:

Who can I encourage and inspire?

What can I do to show love instead of judge their lack of performance?

2 John 1:3 NLT
Grace, mercy, and peace, which come from God the
Father and from Jesus Christ—the Son of the Father—
will continue to be with us who live in truth and love.

How to Survive that Dysfunctional Co-Worker

Dear Coach,

I love my job but I have a co-worker that thinks it is his job to micromanage every project that our team has to do. How do we get him to understand that he is not the boss?

–Just Trying to Do My Work

Dear Just Trying,

We all have coworkers who occasionally, or frequently, drive us up a wall. But, effectively dealing with the difficult behaviors of coworkers will have more to say about **WHO** you are than **HOW** they act. Your reaction to dysfunction will demonstrate your maturity and competence as a valued, contributing employee at work. But it's hard to do what we know is right. **Right?** The first step to peace of mind is to realize we have the freedom to choose our response to any circumstance.

How will you CHOOSE?

1. Avoid or Address

Choose ADDRESS. Peace should be a top priority in any organization. The ability to address and resolve conflict is essential to effectiveness, productivity and profit. Studies reveal a staggering 25 percent of employee time is spent engaging in–or trying to resolve–conflict. When emotions are high, intellect is low.

2. Gossip or Grace
Think about it… which would you rather be the recipient of???
Choose GRACE. The ability to work together in harmony, to extend grace and to resolve inevitable conflicts are indispensable skills to long-term success. However, many organizations are far from peaceful. Instead they are faced with conflict, escalated tension and continual frustration. They are not working together for a common goal; they are in competition with each other.

3. Me or We
Choose WE. By transforming the environment and attitudes to more of a collaborative culture, an organization can achieve systemic and cross-functional global goals while enhancing the personal performance of each team members.

Collaborative Cultures Make a Profitable Difference
We are better than me, is a recipe for success. The challenge for leaders is to concentrate more on creating a culture of **TEAMWORK** that produces more energy than it consumes. When people are focused on individual effort or internal competition it consumes valuable energy. The result of this collaborative culture is a source of competitive advantage. It creates a place that is constantly improving and inspiring ordinary people to do extraordinary things.

"Don't find fault; find a remedy." –Henry Ford

From the Coach:

Unity is often overlooked in the market place because we are trained to compete. But if we look at God's way of doing things we see that where there is unity He commands His blessing.

Ask Yourself:

If God is truly my source then WHO is my competition?

Who can I extend grace to this week?

Instead of seeing fault I will choose to find a solution. Where can I do this?

Forget the former things do not dwell on the past. See, I am doing a new thing! Now it springs up; do you not perceive it? I am making a way in the wilderness and streams in the wasteland. ~ Isaiah 43:18-19

Say No to New Year's Resolutions... Set Goals Instead

Dear Coach,

I set myself up to fail again. I made a list of things I "resolved" to change this year and I have fallen off course. How can I follow through and get the results? – Stuck in Yesterday

Dear Stuck in Yesterday,

The New Year has always been a time of reflection, a time to make a fresh start in the right direction, to resolve to do better, to change! The most popular resolutions are:

- Lose Weight
- Exercise More
- Quit bad habits
- Pay off Debt
- Save More Money
- Spend More Time with Family
- Increase Income
- Go back to School

Resolutions are defined as a "firmness of mind", lots of people make them but studies prove very few follow through only 8% are consistently successful. Here's a New Year's Resolution anyone can keep... Resolve to not make anymore New Year's Resolutions! Try Setting Goals instead!

The ability to set goals has been called the "master skill" for all success. The reason "New Year's Resolutions" typically don't work is because they are based on will power and not life style change over time.

It is reported that only 3% of people have written goals. –Harvard Business School

5 Easy Goal Setting Steps to Achieve Your Desired Results!

1. **Decide what you what to accomplish!** Clarity is key! Make it specific and realistic. For example if you want to lose some extra pounds then decide on a healthy weight that you want to maintain. If you want to pay off debt and save money, then decide on a specific dollar amount.

2. **Write it Down the What and WHY and Make IT Known!** Handwriting is a psycho neuromuscular activity that literally imprints your brain. It helps you visualize the desired outcome. After you write down the "**WHAT**" make a list of the reasons "**WHY**" knowing the why will help you stay focused when it gets tough. **Make IT Known** ... Share with someone the goal. You are far more likely to succeed when you have supporters to inspire your pursuit.

3. **Set a Deadline...** Deadlines may seem stressful but if there is no date then it likely won't happen. Your subconscious mind uses deadlines as "forcing systems" to drive you, consciously and unconsciously toward achieving your goal on schedule. If your goals are huge then set sub-deadlines. If for some reason you don't get to where you want to go by the time you set, don't give up, simply set a new deadline.

4. **Plan and Measure...** Organize your goal into smaller daily action steps. What can you do today or in the next seven days to move closer to completing the goal? Then after the seven days measure where you are in the process.

5. **Commit NOT to Quit!** You will experience obstacles to overcome. *A goal is planned conflict with the status quo!* Setting goals are not meant to be agonizing; they are designed to help you live the life you always dreamed about. By setting meaningful goals, the short term discomfort will be worth the long term benefits of new habits.

From the Coach:

Goals that are not on paper are like seeds without soil!

Ask Yourself:

What are my Goals in every area of my life?

Spiritual
Family
Career
Physical
Social
Intellectual
Financial
Emotional

"Having goals creates excitement and purpose in our life. Focusing on obtaining them instead of looking at current circumstances is how you win everyday. When you consistently live like this then you are living 2 Corinthians 5:7... We live by faith and not by sight."

Top 10 Essentials of a Great Team Player

Dear Coach,
I want to be a better Team Player. How can I improve? - Chosen

Dear Chosen,
Pick ME! Pick ME!!! That reminds me of an elementary school playground where no one wants to be the last person pick for the team. We all want to be indispensable, but what are the "must haves" to get picked as a team player? Are you the person everyone wants on their team?

Teamwork is a key success factor in business, family, church and recreation. But what are the character traits of great team players? We conducted a poll and asked this "If you could choose the ESSENTIAL TRAITS of your Co-Workers and assemble the team around you, what would be MOST important to you?" Here's what we learned...

Top 10 Essentials of Great Team Players
    1. Dependable
    2. Effective Communicator

3. Confident
4. Solution Oriented
5. Adaptable
6. Patient
7. Enthusiastic
8. Competent
9. Disciplined
10. Tenacious

How would you rate in the Team Player Trait Poll? Try taking this **Quick Team Trait Evaluation.**
On a scale from 1 to 10 with 10 being perfect how would you rate yourself?
Your score could increase your draft pick potential. Creating that "Superstar Team" starts with you. Rating you and your co-workers makes a fun staff meeting or team exercise.

Top 10 Quick Team Trait Evaluations
1. Dependable　1　2　3　4　5　6　7　8　9　10
Yours to Count on… Can you be counted on? Dependable people are consistently on time and deliver. They can be trusted to honor their commitments and keep promises. This is a learned behavior that is largely based on self-esteem and core values.

2. Effective Communicator　1　2　3　4　5　6　7　8　9　10
The world's greatest communicators know to incorporate more than words to persuade and inspire people to take action.

3. Confident　1　2　3　4　5　6　7　8　9　10
Confidence precedes results. Team members who are confident about the mission as well as their ability to achieve success will motivate others to higher levels of performance.

4. Solution Oriented   1   2   3   4   5   6   7   8   9   10
Solution oriented people look to resolve issues instead of look for fault.

5. Adaptable   1   2   3   4   5   6   7   8   9   10
Adaptable people are teachable and choose to explore processes, plans and solutions to accomplish the overall team objectives.

6. Patient   1   2   3   4   5   6   7   8   9   10
This essential is evident in the difficult times. When the pressure is on is when our patience is tested. Usually, when we pass this test results in stronger and improved relationships.

7. Enthusiastic   1   2   3   4   5   6   7   8   9   10
Enthusiasm is contagious and enthusiastic people can coach, encourage and inspire the team through rough terrain.

8. Competent   1   2   3   4   5   6   7   8   9   10
Webster's defines it like this… having adequate abilities or capacity to function and develop in a specific skill or qualification.

9. Disciplined   1   2   3   4   5   6   7   8   9   10
Is the ability to get done tasks that you may not "FEEL" like doing! It's self-control gained by enforcing obedience over time.

10. Tenacious   1   2   3   4   5   6   7   8   9   10
Where there is a will there is a way! Tenacious people never give up.

Score Key

81 to 100 Points= Excellent Team Player! First Round Pick
51 to 80 Points= We WILL Keep You… Second Round Pick
0 to 40 Points= Great News these are LEARNED skills… Third Round Pick

From the Coach:

Do you want a loyal and engaged team? The best way is to genuinely believe, encourage and celebrate their dreams.

Ask Yourself:

How can I become a better team player?

Who can I share this survey with?

*Do not despise these small beginnings, for the LORD
rejoices to see the work begin... - Zechariah 4:10*

You Can Make a Difference

Dear Coach,
How can I make a difference and effective positive change if I am not a part of Senior Leadership? −Caught in the Middle

Dear Caught in the Middle,
Most people have felt ineffective in creating positive change based on their role within an organization. There is a common misconception that you can't lead unless you're at the top.

"The truth is leadership is measured by influence."

People often think that leadership comes from having a position or title but real leadership is a development process. This process includes building trust and developing relationships with people who work with you, for you and the leaders above you. Leading from where you are is about increasing your influence at all levels. Influence happens when we grow; personally in character, our relationships with others as well as our professional skill levels. Effecting positive change doesn't come with a title, position or promotion given, it is an inner desire driven by pure motives.

In "Developing the Leader Within You.", John Maxwell outlines what he calls "The Five Levels of Leadership." These leadership principles can be developed at any level of the organization because they focus on individual character and skill.

Maxwell explains **the first level is position**. You don't want to stay at level one for long. This level says people follow you because they have to and this often creates an environment of mistrust and low morale. If this is where you are starting from you can invest time in your followers.

The second level is permission. People are following you because they want to. You have won them over and you have some stated authority.

Level three is production. People are impressed by your performance. They admire what you have done for the organization.

Level four is people development. This is a level where real growth occurs. People follow you because of what you have done for them. They have experienced your commitment to developing others. That commitment will ensure ongoing increase to the organizations success. The people development level will also cause duplication and multiplication.

The fifth level is personhood. This level says people follow you because of who you are and what you represent.

"This level is based on respect developed and proven over time."

The purpose of leading positive change is to accomplish a desired result. Leadership is a choice you make not a place you sit. It is not a reward that someone of importance grants. Every level of an organization is depending on leadership from someone. The desires to innovate, to improve, to create and to find a better way are all characteristics of a leader. You can make a difference no matter where you are on the organizational chart. It has been said that nothing happens until someone provides leadership for it. The key

is to making a difference and effecting positive change is to develop
influence and strengthen relationships at every level.

From the Coach:

You can't teach what you don't live and you can't give what you
don't have. Good news is change is a choice.

Ask Yourself:

What leadership level Am I currently positioned?

What can I do this week to improve my leadership skills?

Don't let anyone think less of you because you are young. Be an example to all believers in what you say, in the way you live, in your love, your faith, and your purity. – 1 Timothy 4:12 NLT

Looking for Rising Stars

Dear Coach,

I am looking for people in our company to take on new levels of responsibility. How can I tell the difference between real substance and the appearance of leadership skills?

–Looking for Rising Stars

Dear Looking for Rising Stars,

Looks can sometimes be deceiving, we see someone who is doing well in their current position and we tap them for promotion. We can get caught up seeing someone who has great intelligence or personality and think they have what it takes to be a great leader. We all have heard someone with an authoritative presences deliver a bold vision that later turned out to be nothing but ego and hot air. Great leaders have more than the appearance of leadership; they know how to get results.

Here are eight attributes for identifying people to be future leaders:

1. The ability to position or reposition–These characteristic surfaces in people who can find ideas for business that meets a consumer need. It is a real asset to find a person with the ability to position or reposition. This kind of leader enables an organization to solve a problem, or answer a

question while being supported by the available market and sustaining a profit.

2. The ability to forecast future market trends–These people can detect patterns and see things others can't. They can think a process through and see possibilities to capitalize the position. This is a skill that can put an organization on the offense in a complex and ever changing world.

3. Aligning the People–Identifying and promoting people with strong social skills, who can align the social system of an organization, will result in increase effectiveness. Imagine having the right people in the optimal positions utilizing their gifts, talents and skills. Couple that with the right behaviors, informed and equipped and you have the making of engaged employees. Informed and engaged employees are able to make better decisions faster. That is the key to achieving greater results–alignment.

4. Evaluating Performance and making necessary changes– Great leaders not only align social systems but they calibrate people based on their actions, decisions and behaviors and match them to the non-negotiable skills of the specific job. They can also evaluate performance based on the overall corporate objectives. Even better is a leader that can see things need to change and take the action to change them.

5. Insisting on Unity–Highly competent people can be a challenge to direct with their ability to be independent thinkers. Their authority figures must have the power to coordinate and shape the team in unity for a common purpose while respecting diversity and individuality. Great leaders insist on unity without uniformity.

6. Setting Long and Short Term Goals–Great leaders have the ability to cast vision and the skills to translate global vision into practical action.

7. Delineate Laser Sharp Focus of Priorities–Often there are so many great ideas and initiatives to launch it is hard to know which one will net the greatest results. Great leaders can

define and chart the course or path by aligning resources, actions and energy to accomplish the desired outcome.

8. Dealing with External Forces beyond the market – Anticipating and responding to societal pressures you don't control but that directly affect your business. A prime example of this is the change in the fast food industry. People today are demanding healthier choices when eating out and as a result that external force has required many fast food chains to change their menus. Great leaders anticipate, address and respond.

There are many behavioral traits that make people shine like a star. When you are looking for future leaders the most important is personal integrity. Without a doubt, intelligence, personality and the ability to communicate are important. People will follow ability and skill for a while, but lasting leadership is built on trust and character. It has been said your ability can never take you where your character can't keep you.

From the Coach:

Often times through trials God will reveal your capacity. We are created by Greatness to be world changers!

Ask Yourself:

Have I judged the people around me fairly?

All Scripture is God-breathed and is useful for teaching, rebuking, correcting and training in righteousness, so that the servant of God may be thoroughly equipped for every good work. 2 Timothy 3:16-17

Strategic Planning

Dear Coach,
Our organization is going through a strategic planning process. What do they mean by vision, isn't that the same as goals? Could you explain the process and define the terms?
–Confused Planner

Dear Confused Planner,
Strategic planning is a systematic way of planning for the future. It is a process of taking informational inputs, organizing that information and then producing an output=THE PLAN. This process is essential to success because it takes strategies, goals and objectives and charts a course that keeps the organization focused and unified. Strategic planning helps determine where you are going and how to get there. There are various methodologies but the outcome is usually a course of action to achieve a desired result. Its purpose will also direct decision making and disperse resources. The foundations of organizational strategic planning are vision, mission, values, goals, and action or execution of the plan.

Vision and Its Impact
The **VISION** is the "where" you are going. Its' purpose is to inspire and direct us toward the future. Eleanor Roosevelt said, "The future belongs to those who believe in the beauty of their dreams." If leaders

fail to dream big dreams, then a company may never attain greatness. We only rise to the level of expectations we see.

Vision should resonate with members of the organization to help them feel proud, excited, and part of something much bigger than themselves. It should also stretch the organization's capabilities and image of itself.

An excellent vision is consistent with the organization's values. In short, a vision should challenge and inspire the group to achieve its mission.

John F. Kennedy did not live to see the reality of his vision for NASA, but he set it in motion when he said, "By the end of the decade, we will put a man on the moon."

That night, when the moon came out, we could all look out the window and imagine. And when it came time to appropriate the enormous funds necessary to accomplish this vision, Congress did not hesitate. Why? Because this vision spoke powerfully to values Americans held dear: America as a pioneer and America as world leader.

Mission Minded
Mission is your organization's fundamental purpose. It's why you exist as a company. For example, The United Way's mission is helping build community capacity for a better quality of life worldwide through voluntary giving and action. Coca-Cola states this mission "To Refresh the World, to inspire moments of optimism and to create value and make a difference. In each instance, the company is built around its mission. Having a mission shapes the organization and its culture. Mission is essential to staying the course. Changes in the market and the economy—as well as lucrative business opportunities—can complicate the ability of an organization to stay true to its identity. A solid mission sounds as a battle cry, bringing unity to all levels of an organization.

Visible Values

Values are the beliefs that govern your behavior as an organization.
One of the most potent tools for making fulfilling life choices is to explore, define and clarify your core values. Our values are the internal compass that helps guide our decision making. When we make decisions based on our values, we feel peace and contentment. Values also define how people behave with each other in the company. They are characteristics as to how the company will value customers, suppliers and the internal community. Values are often the most recognizable of the three. Great companies with great values put their money where their mouth is. In other words, steadfast values yield results in the form of good employee benefit packages, positive community involvement and strong corporate cultures. Values are often the most outward sign for both employees and community of what your company is really all about.

Guiding Goals

Goals are the means or road to the vision, the steps to get there.
Goal: the object to which effort or ambition is directed; the destination of a journey. —Oxford English Dictionary

It's been said that every organization has goals, whether we know what they are or not. An important distinction, however, is that great organizations are very intentional and focused on their goals. Success is in the alignment between the vision, mission, values, goals and actions.

Setting measurable goals can drive your company's competitive advantage... especially if your organization has a number of "stretch goals" it must achieve to insure economic viability or survivability. Without a clear target, you remain in a constant state of instability. While you are going through the motions—all you are doing is running in circles.

Action Plans are the verb of the strategic plan. Action will move you from where you are to where you what to be. Action plans break down complex goals into immediately "do-able" steps. An action plan is simply a list of all the tasks you will need to complete in order to achieve the goal. It is the next step to seeing the vision become a reality. One of the greatest keys to a successful strategic plan is the plan's execution. Action or execution is the "how" of the planning process. When creating a plan include how you intended to carry out the plan. Planning the action and execution pieces will help you to have a more realistic view.

Strategic planning is an essential to organizational success, but it doesn't have to be so complex that it gets left out of our day to day. It is not something that is done once a year and the two inch thick document gets tucked away in a desk drawer. If executed with excellence strategic planning becomes a culture that improves communication, clarifies direction, while establishing a common and shared vision for the organization to pursue. Keeping it simple, communicating and translating the plan into daily action. That is where the power lives.

From the Coach:

Excellence strategic planning becomes a culture that improves communication, clarifies direction, while establishing a common and shared vision for the organization to pursue.

Ask Yourself:

Are my goals and plans clear?

How am I measuring my progress?

As long as the earth remains, there will be planting and harvest, cold and heat, summer and winter, day and night. – Genesis 8:22

Your Most Valuable Asset...

Dear Coach,

I am working longer hours, not eating right and I'm ready to make a change. I'm not happy with the all the weight I have gained and I feel tired all the time. I need the help of an expert!–Tired of Being Tired

Dear Tired of Being Tired,

Your question makes me think of a story I've heard a million times in the years I've worked with Franklin Covey. It's the Aesop's Fable of the Goose and the Golden Egg. In short, the fable tells of a goose that laid golden eggs, bringing the farmers who owned it many riches and much happiness. However, the farmers, in a spirit of capitalizing on their good fortune and in hopes of getting more gold and even richer than they already were, killed the goose in their get-richer-quicker scheme.

If we look at this story and put ourselves in the place of the farmers, the moral is about taking care of our assets and resources. Assets can be many things—both tangible and intangible—from finances, friends, and employees to knowledge, our children, and our talents.

When we max out or neglect any of our resources, their ability to yield a return decreases and ultimately, can cease to exist altogether.

Consider for a second that "YOU" are your most important and valuable asset. What happens if you don't take time for preventative maintenance? How does that impact your ability to produce in every area of your life?

These discoveries may not be revolutionary. They may sound like common sense but I have learned what seems logical is often NOT so common. They are usually easier and more FUN to read about than to actually apply to your life. **The TRUTH is if you don't take care of yourself you can't take care of anyone else.** There has to be a healthy balance. Being a responsible person or having a servant's heart is great if you set boundaries. You cannot ALLOW yourself to get depleted or burnt out. It can cause you to become resentful. Those resentful feelings can manifest into more unhealthy negative behavior.

It was a very challenging time when I realized something HAD to change. I was feeling overwhelmed, overworked, frustrated and out of control by my everyday busy lifestyle. Because I was caring for and managing all the details of family, business and ministry, I didn't slow down long enough to see that I was not taking care of myself. One day in desperation I asked myself this question...

What do I Really NEED to PERFORM at my best and to MAINTAIN a good ATTITUDE?

Here's what I discovered I NEEDED...

1. Quiet Time Alone with God
2. Adequate Sleep
3. Proper Nutrition – Balanced Foods, Fruits and Vegetables, Lean Proteins, Vitamins and Minerals and LIMIT the processed foods and fast food
4. Exercise – Do SOMETHING Everyday... Walk, Run, Strength Training and Cardio
5. Time to Think... Renew my mind and create the space to think creatively helps me to solve problems faster

6. Recreation ... FUN and Social Connection... Like Dinner with Friends, Day Trip to the Beach, Lake or Mountains, Mini Golf, Movies, A Sporting Event, a Festival, Amusement Park or just a road Trip Adventure
7. Brain Training... Learning, I really like Lumosity (Check out the brain training games at lumosity.com) read a book, learn a new skill
8. Strong Relationships... Support System, People to Count on, Family, Church, Group of Friends, a sense of belonging to a community
9. Works that Matters... What I am doing has Purpose, I am Making a Difference in someone's life, That Feeling of Accomplishment
10. To LOVE and to be LOVED! I am NEVER Alone. I am treasured, I am LOVED! Jesus said, "A new command I give you: Love one another. As I have loved you, so you must love one another. By this everyone will know that you are my disciples, if you love one another." – John 13:34-35 (NIV)

From the Coach:

There are natural and spiritual laws that govern us. You will reap what you sow. There is cause and effect and seedtime and harvest.

Personal success precedes public success you can't invert that process any more than you can harvest before you plant.

Ask Yourself:

Do I see myself as my most valuable asset?

What can I start today to ensure a healthier ME tomorrow?

Romans 12:6-8 says, "We have different gifts, according to the grace given us. If a man's gift is prophesying, let him use it in proportion to his faith. If it is serving, let him serve; if it is teaching, let him teach; if it is encouraging, let him encourage; if it is contributing to the needs of others, let him give generously; if it is leadership, let him govern diligently; if it is showing mercy, let him do it cheerfully."

NO FEAR!

Dear Coach,
I have been invited to speak to a group of people. I am excited about the opportunity but I am really nervous. Do you have any tips for giving a great presentation?
–Bundle of Nerves

Dear Bundle of Nerves,
Feeling nervous before giving a presentation or speech is natural. It demonstrates your desire to do well. Being successful in public speaking is often measured by the connection between you, your audience and the message. When we speak our goal is to transfer information, empower change, create awareness and inspire or encourage. Often the challenge is to create an environment that fosters action after your presentation.

Here are a few tips for giving a great presentation:

Passion
There is a zeal that shines through a presenter's face when he or she is speaking on a topic they have passion for. That zeal is also seen when

there is a passion for people and a deep desire to make a difference in the lives they encounter. Think of something you believe in so strongly that you are immoveable, something you live, that should be your message. Delivering a message you are passionate about will also give you confidence that you have something valuable to share.

As author and business guru Tom Peters said, "Forget all the conventional rules but one. There is one golden rule: Stick to topics you deeply care about, and do not keep your passion buttoned inside your vest. An audience's biggest kick is the speaker's obvious enthusiasm. If you are lukewarm about the issue, then forget it."

Prepare the Message and the Audience

Great presentations take time. On average speakers spend one hour for every minute they speak. This time includes asking questions, getting to know who the audience is as well as preparing the content. If you research all you can about the audience in front of you, when you share things that relate to them it brings warmth and increases their interest. A great place to start is to ask this question, "What is the desired outcome of this presentation?" It is equally important to know your materials. If you are uncomfortable with them your nervousness will increase. Practice is a requirement. Rehearse the entire presentation and make adjustments as needed. Only in speaking out loud will you discover where the gaps are and how the transitions flow. Speaking or presenting is actually structured conversation with a focused point. An audience comes into a presentation asking, "Why am I here?" Your job is to give them something they can use. If you are successful they will leave asking, "How do I implement these ideas?"

"We are not the superstars, our audience is. We are not the center of attention, the message is." –Connie Podesta

Arrive Early

Arriving early to get familiar with the space and to test all audio and visual equipment can reduce the level of anxiety. If you are using

PowerPoint go through all the slides. If there is a video, make sure you play it in its' entirety. Walk around in the place you will be presenting and practice using the microphone and any other visual aids.

Greet People

Introduce yourself to some of the audience prior to your presentation. Being interested in them will take the focus off of yourself and this will help you to relax. It is less intimidating to speak to people you know.

Relax

Relax by taking slow, deep breaths. Imagine yourself presenting, your tone is clear and assured, you are confident and charming. When you see yourself as successful that is what your audience will see. During your presentation don't apologize or make excuses for being nervous, you may be calling attention to something the audience had not realized. The audience has granted you authority and there is a level of credibility and trust given to you. It is up to you to take it. Remember that your audience wants you to succeed. They are on your side and cheering for you.

From the Coach:

God has not given us a spirit of fear but of power, and of love, and of a sound mind. Boldness comes from knowing and trusting GOD'S word.

Ask Yourself:

Am I allowing fear to keep me from pursuing God's purpose for my life?

What is the worst thing that could happen if I stepped up and spoke?

Don't be fooled by those who say such things, for "bad company corrupts good character." - 1 Corinthians 15:33

Experiencing Superior Service Leads to Demonstrating

Dear Coach,

I'm a leader who understands excellent customer service is fundamental to success. Keeping customers consistently coming back and happy is critical. There are gaps between what I believe to be good customer service and what my direct reports believe. What can I do to better equip my staff?

–People Person

Dear People Person,

How may I help you? Oh, the question that puts a smile on your face. As leaders and business owners, our livelihood depends on how well we answer that question. The Stanford Research Institute found, "The money you make in any endeavor is determined by only 12.5% knowledge and 87.5% by your ability to deal with people. In today's market, with so many choices, it is not enough just to give the customer what they want. We must also anticipate what they don't know they want and provide service that WOWS. So, why do customers leave? Research reveals 1% Die, 3% Move away, 5% Other friendships, 9% Competitive reasons, 14% Product dissatisfaction, and 68% leave because of an attitude of indifference toward them by an employee. There seems to be a gap in service mentality nowadays. Some employees seem to be disengaged, viewing their work performance separate from the organizations overall success, when in fact it is directly connected.

Serving customers should be seen as an opportunity, rather than an obligation.

Here are a few suggestions for taking customer service to the new levels:

1. Ask the Customer
Knowledge is a powerful tool that propels business success. Having knowledge about how customers see our business allows us to make positive changes. When we know the truth it also helps to increase the speed of that change. Ask customers for honest feedback and embrace the truth. It may not always be what you expected.
Here are a few great questions to ask:

- Why did your customers originally choose to do business with you?
- Why do existing clients continue to do business with you?
- How would your customers rate their overall level of satisfaction with your business?
- According to your clients, what do you do well?
- According to your clients how could you improve?
- Do your current clients know what other products and services you offer?
- What could you do to get more business from your existing customer base?
- What additional products or services would your clients like for you to offer?
- Would your current clients be confident in referring business to you?

Answering these questions can also help to establish a benchmark for training staff. It will provide information and clearly identify performance gaps. At the same time, you may find new business strategies to generate growth and increase. Knowing your customers is essential to long term growth. Today's customers can be impatient and demanding. They have high expectations and very little time. Top performing companies are always looking for ways to speed up and improve service. To get feedback about customers needs, Lexus started an Owner's Advisory Forum in 1998. For Lexus, communication can be especially challenging considering manufacturers are in Japan and the majority of customers are in the United States. Each year Lexus brings about 20 engineers who are responsible for design and production, and they meet with 15 to 20 loyal Lexus owners. Together they talk about the details of the car, what they like and what they dislike. As a result Lexus customers have grown from 500,000 to over one million. Lexus dealers have also earned highest honors in customer satisfaction from J.D. Power and Associates for eight of the past nine years.

2. Define Superior Customer Service

During our customer service workshops one of the first things we do is define superior customer service. What exactly does that mean to you? Most people have never thought that our customers are just like us. When we think of service we tend to think of how we have been served and not how we serve. We view customer service from our own perspective. As an organization it is critical to expand those personal experiences by communicating, not only verbally but in visual and kinesthetic ways, specifically what we expect our employees to deliver. I have heard it said, **"When you hear something, you may forget it. When you see something, you will remember it. But not until you do something, will you understand it."** We should treat our customers as we want to be treated but until we experience superior customer service for ourselves, we may not understand what it takes to provide that level of service.

"When you hear something, you may forget it. When you see something, you will remember it. But not until you do something, will you understand it."

3. People Development: Character and Skill

Superior customer service requires character and skill. It can be defined by delivering the unexpected. We expect people to be friendly. We expect at best an average level of service. The average work environment isn't terrible; it's average. And consequently, good is the enemy of great. To get people to deliver superior customer service, we need to look at two areas, the development of character and the training of skills. People who demonstrate superior customer service have a genuine passion for serving people. They remember the customers' preferences, pay attention to the details, know their products and services and exceed expectations.

From the Coach:

Successful people are always taking personal inventory and continually working on improving themselves.

Ask Yourself:

What is the BEST customer experience that I have ever had?

What can I do to improve how I deal with people?

*Gently instruct those who oppose the truth. Perhaps
God will change those people's hearts, and they
will learn the truth. - 2 Timothy 2:25 NLT*

Inspiring Change

Dear Coach,
Our organization has always been reluctant to change and now our
bottom line is suffering. Our systems are outdated and employee
morale is low. We need to change our focus and redirect our efforts
before it's too late. How can we move forward?
–Changing Times

Dear Changing Times,
As a leader deciding to make organizational, structural or strategic
changes to keep up with the changing market place is the easy
part. It is much more challenging to convince people to get on
board or follow your lead. Change is not easy, but it is required.
Things are always changing; just take a look at nature. Our world is
continually going through the process of change and growth. You
may have heard the saying, "Growth without change is impossible."
We can't expect sustained growth without being consistent in our
development. We can't always control change but we can control
our responds to it. Why is it so hard to embrace change? Change is
an emotional process. We are creatures of habit who usually resist
change and welcome routine. The unknown or uncertain can be
scary. I have heard it said that when old patterns or habits are broken
then new and better worlds emerge.

Staying the same leads to mediocrity and these days mediocre organizations won't survive long. I believe change is the key that can unlock doors of growth, efficiency, increase profit and engaged employees. Our job is to convince our team that the "new world" we are trying to create is better than the one we are currently operating in. Here are a few tips for inspiring change:

1. **Begin by letting go outdated beliefs.** Walk away and forget about how we have always done things, and then ask, how we can more efficiently achieve our desired results. Peter Drucker said, "It is easier for companies to come up with new ideas than to let go of old ones."

2. **Be honest and evaluate your current position.** Change what needs changing and not what is easy to change.

3. **Ask your best people to tell you what they think.** Before the completion of your "New World", new vision, direction or organizational change, get your brightest and best people involved in the planning process. "A good leader inspires people to have confidence in their leader. A great leader inspires people to have confidence in themselves." –Anonymous

4. **Past Success does not guarantee future success.** We often hold on to the outdated methods because they brought us success at one time. Our once valid beliefs and practices may have outlived their usefulness. Innovation is the secret to winning the race.

5. **Simplify your message.** I recently read a story about Roberto Goizueta, the former CEO of Coca-Cola. In 1979, Goizueta was promoted to president, and then in 1981 became the company's chairman. During that sixteen year span, it is reported that Goizueta created more wealth for shareholders than any CEO in the company's history. And made Coca-Cola the most prominent trademark in the world. Roberto's success is attributed to his ability to encapsulate complex ideas and present them in a concise and compelling style. He

was best known for his often repeated description of Coke's infinite growth potential. He said, "Each of the six billion people on this planet consumes on average sixty-four ounces of fluids daily, of which only two ounces are Coca-Cola." Closing the sixty-two ounce gap became the centerpiece of inspiration and motivation within the company. Simple message, extraordinary results.

From the Coach:

Change is the catalyst for growth and progress! Don't resist it. Embrace it! It's your answer.

Ask Yourself:

What are some of the out-dated mind sets, habits or processes that are hindering my growth?

"Prayer operates under the principle of sowing and reaping. When you pray for someone else don't be surprised that what you prayed shows up in your own life." Read James 5:13-19

Do You Trust Me?

Dear Coach,
Our company is going through a challenging time. There are rumors and fears about the future. Our management team needs help to get things back on track and increase production.
–Stakeholder in Limbo

Dear Stakeholder,
Change and uncertainty often fosters an environment of fear which leads to a lack of trust. The lack of trust can slow things down and create higher cost of doing business. Building trust and restoring confidence can significantly impact bottom line results.

"Our distrust is very expensive" –Ralph Waldo Emerson

Keys to Building Trust
1. Communicate honestly
2. Show respect
3. Be transparent
4. Show loyalty
5. Keep commitments
6. Clarify expectations
7. Be accountable
8. Extend Trust

Communicate Honestly
Be Honest. In communication talk straight. Tell the truth. Let people know where they stand and demonstrate integrity. When we manipulate people or distort the facts it destroys relationships as well as our own self image. Spinning the truth or leaving false impressions carries the same consequences. Confront issues and address challenges quickly.

Show Respect
This behavior is the Golden Rule in action. This rule is recognized by almost every culture and religion worldwide. What is the impact of speed and cost as it results to respect? Showing respect directly results in bottom line growth. One of the most powerful ways to show respect is to listen and understand another person's point of view or position.

Be Transparent
Be real, open and honest especially about motives and decisions. Surveys suggest that the first key to restoring public trust is a "spirit of transparency." We are not being transparent when we withhold information, have hidden agendas or cover up.

Show Loyalty
There are many ways to show loyalty. Acknowledging people for a job well done or giving credit for an idea or solution will significantly increase trust and economic results. Also be loyal to the absent, talking about people when they are not present only destroys your own credibility.

Keep Commitments
Keeping commitments may have the greatest impact on trust. In a study on business ethics "keeping promises" ranked the number one behavior in creating an ethical culture. This may sound like common sense but it is not always common practice. Never over promise and under deliver.

Clarify Expectations

To be clear about expectations we need to create a shared out come and agree about what is to be done–up front. This action can prevent frustration in the future. Clarifying expectations must be mutual, collaborative and agreed upon. We should never assume that expectations are clear or understood by everyone.

Be Accountable

Being accountable means taking responsibility or ownership. Accountability begins with us as we take responsibility for results and are clear about our expectations. When we are accountable we don't blame or point fingers, we look for solutions.

Extending Trust is a powerful motivator

There is nothing that motivates or inspires people like having trust extended to them. When trust is extended, people don't need to be managed they manage themselves. Extending trust is based on the principles of empowerment, reciprocity, and a fundamental belief that people are capable of being trusted. On the other hand people tend not to trust people who don't trust them.

The truth is in every relationship–professional or personal–your actions or what you do has far greater impact than anything you say. You can say you respect someone but unless you demonstrate that respect through your actions, your words become meaningless.

"The only way to build trust is by being trustworthy." –Gerard Arpey

From the Coach:

Fear causes people to fabricate but clear and transparent communication brings peace. Don't be defensive and withhold information when asked to prove yourself.

Ask Yourself:

Do I limit myself because I don't trust people?

How can I learn to trust God and forgive people?

Be still, and know that I am GOD! I will be honored by every nation. I will be honored throughout the world. ~ Psalm 46:10

The Winning Edge

Dear Coach,

Our company is operating as lean as possible but unfortunately we have experienced some layoffs. How can I secure my position within the organization?

–Looking for Security

Dear Looking for Security,

Most people think they can add value or obtain job security by impressing the boss with a "BIG WIN." There is another way of thinking that suggests winning happens in the attention to details. The "Winning Edge" is a concept that says, "Small differences in ability, performance, process or detail can lead to enormous differences in results." In one year of the Olympic Games the margin of victory for the Men's 200 meter Freestyle swimming event was only 1.42 seconds and for the Women's 200 meter Freestyle, .59 seconds. Over the last twenty-five years in all the major golf tournaments the margin of victory combined was less than three strokes. That three stroke winning difference equated to a 76% difference in take home prize money between first and second place.

"The Winning Edge says Success is in the details and Everything Counts!"

In the majority of competitions there are usually only fractions separating the decision of victory. The same is true for "winning" in business. It is attention to detail, building relationships and innovation that sets people apart. As participants in this fast-paced and uncertain global market we must always be improving our performance. It has been said, "The magic behind every outstanding performance is always found in the smallest of details."

Giving Just Enough to Get By?

Success leaves no room for giving just enough to get by. Sam Parker and Mac Anderson shared this example of "Extra Effort" At 211 degrees, water is hot... At 212 degrees, it boils. Raising the temperature of water by one extra degree means the difference between something that is simply very hot and something that generates enough force to power a machine—a beautiful, uncomplicated metaphor that ideally should feed every endeavor—consistently pushing us to make the extra effort in every task we undertake. It reminds us that seemingly small things can make tremendous differences.

Most people long to accomplish great tasks, but even the biggest project depends on the success of the smallest parts. We tend to focus on the big picture, which is important. People often dismiss small details, while in fact our whole ecosystem is simply an accumulation of tiny details. Think about the tiny seeds that produce the abundant harvest in the fall or the stability of a downtown twenty story building. The integrity of the structure could be threatened by the smallest element. This same principle applies to all areas of business.

There is a science behind every outstanding performance, great relationship, luxury car, custom home, exceptional meal, or fine piece of furniture, it is a craftsmanship found in the details.

Some believe they are too busy to focus on details, or that attending to the 'minutia' of your career or business would make you less effective in producing superior products and services. When the details are neglected often organizations are challenged by greater problems. The details of everyday work affect the ability to compete and prosper.

Organizations are holding on to individuals who understand that very small differences, consistently practiced, produce superior results. Successful people know that everything counts.

Today's "Winning Edge" is consistent attention to details produces excellence, and often job security.

From the Coach:

You can try to out run the storm or stand in the rain. Some would say run, get out of the rain silly but there is something liberating and refreshing about being still and letting the storm pass. Don't limit today by assuming the same outcome as yesterday. Expecting the best will bring the best. True security comes from knowing and trusting God as your source.

Ask Yourself:

Am I really giving my best?

Where do I need to give more focus?

Pressure Shortens the Fuse

Dear Coach,

There is so much drama and arguing, why can't we just get along? I am frustrated by many of our staff as they continue to stir up trouble. I just want harmony at work. This is creating a stressful environment. I need solutions!

–Short Fuse

Dear Short Fuse,

Increase pressure and challenge can cause us to react adversely. When people are drained emotionally it causes them to lash out. Often this rage is caused by hurt, fear or frustration. Hurt is most often produced by vague expectations or jealousy–which leads to anger, resentment and revenge. Workplace anger is costly in time, mistakes, stress, morale, performance and customer service, not to mention the physical consequences of the angry person. The ability to address and defuse conflict is essential to effectiveness, productivity and profit. Studies reveal a staggering 25 percent of employee time is spent engaging in–or trying to resolve–conflict. When emotions are high, intellect is low.

Common Responses to Conflict

People respond to conflict in three ways: Explosion, implosion or resolution. The preferred response is resolution. The ability to work together in harmony and to resolve inevitable conflicts are indispensable skills to long-term success. Below are some suggestions for creating harmony at work. Following these simple steps will save time and resources when things arise.

Five Steps to a Peaceful Work Environment

Step One: People are Priority

Make good relationships first priority: Relationships with people are more important than who wins. Do your best to be courteous to one-another and remain constructive under pressure. It is helpful to understand that the conflict may be a mutual problem, which may be best resolved through discussion and negotiation rather than through raw aggression.

- Listen first; talk second: To solve a problem effectively you have to understand where the other person is coming from before defending your own position.

Step Two: Gather Information

Keep people and problems separate: Recognize that in many cases the other person is not just "being difficult"—real and valid differences can lie behind conflictive positions. By separating the problem from the person, real issues can be debated without damaging working relationships.

By using active listening skills you can ensure you hear and understand other's positions and perceptions.

Also, try to understand the conflict in objective terms: Is it affecting work performance? damaging the delivery? disrupting team work? hampering decision-making? and so on. Be sure to focus on the issues and leave personalities out of the discussion.

Step Three: Agree on the Problem

This sounds like an obvious step, but often different underlying needs, interests and goals can cause people to perceive problems very differently. You'll need to agree the problems that you are trying to solve before you'll find a mutually acceptable solution. Set out the "Facts": Agree and establish the objective, observable elements that will have an impact on the decision.

Step Four: Brainstorm Possible Solutions

Explore options together: Be open to the idea that a third position may exist, and that you can get to this idea jointly. If everyone is going to feel satisfied with the resolution, it will help if everyone has had fair input in generating solutions. Brainstorm possible solutions, and be open to all ideas, including ones you never considered before.

Step Five: Negotiate a Solution

By this stage, the conflict may be resolved: Both sides may better understand the position of the other, and a mutually satisfactory solution may be clear to all. However you may also have uncovered real differences between your positions. This is where a technique like win-win negotiation can be useful to find a solution that, at least to some extent, satisfies everyone.

There are three guiding principles here: **Be Calm, Be Patient, Have Respect.**

Key Points

Conflict can be incredibly destructive to good teamwork.

Managed in the wrong way, real and legitimate differences between people can quickly spiral out of control, resulting in situations where co-operation breaks down and the team's mission is threatened. To calm these situations down, it helps to take a positive approach to conflict resolution, where discussion is courteous and non-confrontational, and the focus is on issues rather than on individuals. When we honor people by listening carefully and explore facts, issues and possible solutions properly, conflict can often be resolved effectively.

From the Coach:

Two things define you, your patience when you have nothing and your attitude when you have everything.

Ask Yourself:

What do I want more... to be right? To have the last word? OR to value people and pursue peace?

Say Yes to What Matters Most!

Dear Coach,
I am struggling with setting boundaries and finding balance in my work and personal life. There are not enough hours in the day. What can you suggest to increase energy and reduce panic?
–Out of Balance

Dear In Search of Balance,
Finding balance in today's frantic-paced world is no easy task. We are addicted to the whirlwind of busyness. There is an increased pressure to do more with less. Maybe you have experienced this seemingly out of control frustration and anxiety that accompanies endless phone calls, voicemails, emails, social media, deadlines, appointments and the list goes on. Most often our greatest discomfort comes from over committing. By saying yes to everything, it is nearly impossible to keeping promises and honor commitments.

Work/life balance is a real issue for people. Boundaries of work and personal lives are often blurred due to our global economy and advanced technology. With Droids, Blackberries, iPhones and wireless connections, people have the ability to work anywhere and we do, even on vacation. Being so connected can have challenges. These challenges can be overcome by applying timeless principles, creating a clear vision and realistic boundaries.

Balance is serious, intentional and purposeful living. It's not for the weak. It takes a highly effective, courageous person to live what matters most. Often it is easy to let life control you. In order to make positive, long lasting impact we need to examine our current habits. Habits are patterns of behavior that consist of three components: desire, knowledge and skill. Habits are created over time. Samuel Smile said, "Sow a thought, reap an action; Sow an action, reap a habit; Sow a habit, reap a character; Sow a character, reap a destiny." Consider making a list of your top ten priorities, then evaluate where you send most of your time. Are your habits and actions in alignment with your highest priorities?

Here are some "Highly Effective Habits" to consider in the search for a balanced life, based on the work of Dr. Steven R. Covey, author of The 7 Habits of Highly Effective People.

<u>Habit 2 Begin with the End in Mind. This is the Habit of Vision</u>

Ineffective: I live by default.
Vs.
Effective: I live by design.

Mental creation precedes physical creation. Beginning with the end in mind will result in a clear definition of where you want to be. The vision provides criteria for deciding what is or is not important. As we start to model this way of thinking, we begin to envision outcomes before we take action, which in turn increases our focus and production.

<u>Habit 3 Put First Things First. This is the Habit of Integrity and Execution</u>

Ineffective: I put urgent things first.
Vs.
Effective: I put important things first.

"Things which matter most must never be at the mercy of things which matter least."
–Johann Goethe

This habit means we are walking our talk. Our actions line up with what we say is important to us. E.M. Gray said it this way, "Successful people have the habit of doing what the unsuccessful don't like to do." Then he added, "They don't like doing them either. But their disliking is subordinated to the strength of their purpose."

Keep in mind that changing habits takes personal commitment. When a rocket is launched it expends more fuel and energy in the first few minutes of lift off than it uses over the next several days to travel a half-million miles. Like gravity, habits have tremendous pull.

Suggestions to Improve Your Overall Effectiveness.
Decide What is Important... Having a clear vision will help in living a balanced life. Balance looks different based on what matters most and the roles you play in your life as well as your objectives. Assess your habits, priorities, objectives and actions.

Plan... Schedule the First things First, but don't over schedule. Decide what needs to be done now and what can wait until later.

Set Boundaries... Determine a set time to shut things down in the evening and focus on your family. If possible eat dinner together or scheduling a family night. If you are single make time for friends. We are social creatures and were made to interact.

Take Care of Yourself... It is important to plan time for self care. Include your whole self, spirit, mind and body. Including personal development or learning new skills can expand your thinking to produce desired results. You are your greatest asset, without you what is there?

Laughter is Good Medicine... Lighten up and laugh.

Just Say No... Be honest and don't over commit. You can't be everywhere all the time. Know when it is OKAY to say No.

What we feed grows and what we starve dies. If we are addicted to being busy, it can give us a false sense of accomplishment. But it is really about our purpose, we achieve balance when our actions are in alignment with our values. Victor Frankl said, "When we can no longer change a situation, we are challenged to change ourselves."

From the Coach:

"We discover rather than invent our purpose in life." - Victor Frankl

It is knowing our purpose and placing priority on living that purpose that truly sets us free.

Ask Yourself:

Am I saying YES to what is really important in life?

But whatever I am now, it is all because God poured out his special favor on me—and not without results. For I have worked harder than any of the other apostles; yet it was not I but God who was working through me by his grace. - 1 Corinthians 15:10

Reward the Results!

Dear Coach,
Our company has fallen short of last quarter's goals. Our leadership team is dedicated and passionate about the success of our organization. We have a strategic plan. We are questioning how this happened and how we get back on track? Do you have any suggestions?
–Lack of Results

Dear Lack of Results,
I like the saying, "Honey Bees get praised while mosquitoes get swatted." It is easy to look busy but what is actually being produced is a good question. Often the missing link between plans and results is execution. Strategy cannot be effectively planned without taking into account how to execute. Surprisingly the inability to execute is common in organizations of all sizes. We get side tracked with the day to day activities and miss the strategic mark. Or on the other end of the scale, we have a good number of high level thinkers who are not interested in the "how" of getting things done. There is a balance between strategic thinking and execution of results.

According to Dun and Bradstreet businesses in America fail due to lack of execution of the most important goals. We need to work toward the "right goals" that net the "right results".

Some of the greatest leaders have an instinct for execution, not only can they see the big picture but they can see step by step what needs to happen to hit the mark. Unfortunately that instinct has not been cultivated in others or taught in the organization. For some it is difficult to make the connection in realizing the scope of what needs to be done to translate vision into specific tasks.

For example, when leaders are detached from subordinates their expectations may trend to be unrealistic. Leaders may not think to involve them with the plan of execution. As a result they are not equipped to deal with unexpected issues and strategies commonly fail.

The solution is to establishing a culture of execution that includes communication and accountability at all levels. Execution produces results when it is woven into the business. It becomes the driving force of the reward system and becomes the behavior that is practiced.

Execution is a discipline that equals growth and results. Execution can be development, not only in leaders but in every person in the organization.

In the New York Times Bestseller, Execution by Larry Bossidy and Ram Charan, they define execution as a systematic process of rigorously discussing "hows" and "whats", questioning, tenaciously following through and ensuring accountability.

Creating an Execution Culture

1. **Alignment** is essential to creating the framework for execution. It is the ability to clearly define priorities to maximize results as well as interrelate people, strategy and operations. Some organizations have no idea if what they do day to day are the activities that really drive the bottom line in a positive way. These companies are gambling with their future prosperity. Long term success comes from alignment and having the right people doing the right job.

2. **Set clear goals and priorities.** Leaders who execute focus on very few clear priorities. When you focus on a few priorities (three to four) you will typically produce the best results.

3. **Ask clarifying questions.** Don't assume you know. Ask all levels of the organization for input as to what needs to be done to obtain the desired results.

4. **Consistency and follow through.** Clear, simple goals mean very little if nobody takes them seriously. Inconsistency and the lack of follow through are small foxes that will destroy the vine. Leaders who are consistent and follow through cultivate trust and results.

5. **Reward the doers.** If you expect people to produce specific results then you must reward those accordingly. Most organizations don't do a good job of linking performance to rewards.

6. **Be realistic.** It is important to be realistic when establishing a culture that executes. Many organizations have people who try to get ahead by over promising. Being realistic will play a key role in building your team and arriving at your desire destination.

From the Coach:

Frustration is what happens either when you DON'T know what to do OR you know what to do and DON'T do it!

Ask Yourself:

Are my goals clear?

Am I realistic?

Don't love money; be satisfied with what you have. For God has said, "I will never fail you. I will never abandon you." - Hebrews 13:5

The Secret to Saving Money!

Dear Coach,

I really want to purchase a condo within the next few years but I am really having trouble with saving money for my down payment. Can you tell me how to get my savings to grow?
–Little Saved-Need A Lot

Dear Little Saved,

Have you ever said, "I will save money when I get more money?" Here's the truth... You will NOT save money when you get that next raise. You will not save money when that car is paid off. You will not save money when the kids are grown. Saving money is NOT a matter 0of math but of emotion...

You will only save money when it becomes an emotional priority.

How would you pay for an unexpected repair or expense? Do you have an emergency fund? Some people said they would borrow from family or friends, sell something or get a loan from the bank but 67% of Americans said that they would use a credit card to cover it. This money mind set will actually compound the crisis, now it's a repair or expense and a financial emergency. According to *Money Magazine*, **78% of Americans will have a major negative financial event in any given 10-year period.**

We all know we need to save, but most people don't save like they know they need to save. Why? Because having it NOW is a competing goal. The goal to save isn't a high enough priority to delay that purchase of the thing we really need, like the latest technical gadget, or that vacation escape. Our desire to spend is also linked to the desire to please the people in our life. So we purchase, buy, consume all our dollars or go into debt to buy things. That debt means monthly payments that control our paychecks and make us say things like, "We just don't make enough to save any money!" Not true! We *do* make enough to save money; we just aren't willing to quit indulging ourselves with our little projects or pleasures to have enough to have any to save. **It doesn't matter what you make—you can save money.** It just has to become a big enough priority to you.

Top 3 Secrets to Successful Saving
#1 Make it Automatic...Have a percentage of every paycheck automatically drafted and deposited into a savings account.

#2 Live on a Budget... Living on a budget will help make savings a priority and a habit. Practice the SAVE NOW Buy Later Principle instead of Buy Now PAY Later **and get rid of unnecessary expenses.**

#3 Start Now even if you Start Small make saving a habit ... Get a PIGGY BANK!

Facts...
Only 1 out of 3 Americans have a savings account.

88% of graduating college seniors has credit-card debt before they even have a job.

90% of people in our culture purchase things they can't afford.
Savings Example... A $4 beverage from Starbucks every morning before work may not seem like a lot, but if you take that $4 and save it for just a month, you'll have about $85!

From the Coach:

Saving money is like depositing peace and security into your future.

Ask Yourself:

What can I live without to start saving more money?

*The Lord is gracious and compassionate; slow
to anger and rich in love. - Psalm 145:8*

That's Not What I SAID!!!

Dear Coach,
I find myself saying, "That is not what I meant." I'm having trouble being understood. My co-workers often walk away frustrated. I thought I had been helpful with advice, but have heard people say that I am rude, insensitive, and a know-it-all. I need tips on improving my communication skills.
–Misunderstood

Dear Misunderstood,
A large part of success is determined by our ability to communicate effectively with others. Many times what you are trying to say isn't heard the way you intended. There is power in the words we use, as well as the delivery of those words or our communication style. You might remember the saying, "Sticks and stones may break my bones, but words will never hurt me." That is far from the truth. The five tips below are designed to improve your communication skills.

Choose Your Words
We might not always be aware that some of the words we use are poison. It has been said that life and death are in the power of the tongue. Words such as "should," "must," "have to" and "ought to" can leave us feeling manipulated. People generally respond to this by withdrawing and shutting down the lines of communication. Skilled communicators are aware of the effect of the words they use.

We reap what we sow, even in dialogue. When we speak positively, we reap positive rewards. When we speak encouragingly, we receive encouragement. The opposite is true as well. Not only do words hurt, but they also can carry consequences. Some hold onto words and comments spoken until it becomes a belief. It is advantageous to choose our words and speak carefully to each other, as well as to ourselves.

Listen to Understand
Effective communicators listen primarily to understand the other person's viewpoint. Most people listen while thinking of their reply, and don't take the time and effort to listen to understand. When we listen to understand, we have greater influence with others and are able to solve complex problems with clarity and speed.

A recent study identified the benefits for those who learn to listen. Good listeners are more respected because they have demonstrated concern for others. They also are better informed because active listening results in greater learning. On the contrary, people who do not listen well find few who are willing to share useful information with them.

Listening to understand is listening without your own agenda. It has been called listening with your heart, or empathic listening. When using this communicative technique, you reflect what a person is saying and feeling in your own words and are not listening to advise, fix, or judge.

The quickest way to defuse a hostile communication is by listening to the other person with the intent to understand them. Being heard instantly builds confidence and trust. Proverbs 15:1 says, "A gentle answer turns away wrath, but a harsh word stirs up anger."

So why is it so difficult to listen? We think four times faster than we can speak, so it takes concentrated patience to listen. When our thoughts race ahead of what is being said, we can get sidetracked and miss important information. One way to improve the odds of listening attentively is to lean forward and focus on the person speaking.

Replace Advice with Questions

Instead of advising—or assuming you know the answer—ask a question. This will bring clarity to a conversation. Open-ended questions cannot be answered with a simple "yes" or "no," and they encourage the speaker to expand on his or her thoughts. Being genuinely curious will affirm your interest in the person and topic.

Expect Value

The best communicators are expecting to hear something great. They are optimistic listeners who expect the speaker to have something beneficial to say. They hang on every word and expect to find truth, insight, and wisdom.

Read the Signs

Communication includes what is being said, as well as what is not being said.

Words we use make up only about 7 percent of what is being communicated, while 38 percent is how we say it through tone and style, and the remaining 55 percent is body language and nonverbal expressions.

A lot can be observed from paying attention to the other person's posture and facial expressions. Slowing down, choosing words, asking questions, taking the time to listen with the intent to understand, expecting value to be spoken and reading the signs will serve well in communicating with others.

From the Coach:

The quickest way to defuse a hostile communication is by listening to the other person with the intent to understand them. Being heard instantly builds confidence and trust. Proverbs 15:1 says, "A gentle answer turns away wrath, but a harsh word stirs up anger."

Ask Yourself:

How well do I listen?

Do I listen to understand the other person or do I listen to respond?

Have confidence in your leaders and submit to their authority, because they keep watch over you as those who must give an account. Do this so that their work will be a joy, not a burden, for that would be of no benefit to you. - Hebrews 13:17

Business Coaching— Unleash Your Potential

Dear Coach,
Our company is ready to get to the next level of success. We are exploring the idea of hiring a business coach. What is business coaching and what should we expect from working with a coach?
–Next Level Leader

Dear Next Level Leader,
Business Coaching is much like sports coaching. A sports coach pushes an athlete to achieve optimum performance. The greatest athletes and teams have great coaches. These coaches know that in order to perform at full potential, they must be able to assess the athlete and structure a plan or regimen that will assist them in gaining the physical and mental skills needed to perform at their highest level.

Business Coaching allows us to assess the current position, to look at where we are but more importantly where we what to be. Like an outstanding sports coach with a winning game plan, the role of a Business Coach is to guide you to a level of success you have never experienced.

Who Has A Coach?

"Who exactly seeks out a coach?" asked an article in the Chicago Tribune, and their answer was: "Winners who want even more out of life."

And in coaching everyone's a winner. For instance, there are coaches who help businesses with organizational development, corporate culture, strategic planning, marketing, team building, leadership development, time management, customer service, goals, transition and focus.

There are also coaches who assist leaders and individuals with public speaking, communication, ADD/ADHD, eliminating debt, changing careers or behavior, giving up bad habits, fitness and parenting.

Benefits of Coaching

Professional Coaching is a partnership that supports the achievement of extraordinary results. Whether business or personal, through the process of coaching, people focus on the skills and actions needed to successfully move from where they are to where they desire to be.

"Executives and HR managers know coaching is the most potent tool for inducing lasting organizational and personal change." -Ivy Business Journal

"Executive coaches are not for the meek," said FAST COMPANY magazine. "They're for people who value unambiguous feedback. All great coaches have one thing in common; it's that they are ruthlessly results-oriented."

"I never cease to be amazed at the power of the coaching process to draw out the skills or talents that were previously hidden within an individual or organization," said John Russell, Managing Director of Harley-Davidson Europe, Ltd., "and coaching invariably finds a way to solve a problem previously though unsolvable."

According to CNN.com, Business Coaching, it's becoming quite the thing. "Once used to bolster troubled staffers, coaching now is part of the standard leadership development training for elite executives and talented up-and-comers at IBM, Motorola, J.P.Morgan, Chase, and Hewlett Packard. These companies are discreetly giving their best prospects what star athletes have long had: a trusted adviser to help reach their goals."

As companies come to realize that people are their most important asset, that people make money, not businesses, the idea of coaching has taken hold. "The goal of coaching is the goal of good management: to make the most of an organization's valuable resources." –Harvard Business Review

Business Coaching accelerates progress by providing greater focus and awareness of possibilities leading to more effective choices. Coaching concentrates the organization on the desired results.

Why Business Coaching Works?
Business Coaching works because it relies on one of the most powerful forces in the world: the power of the social contract and commitment. We try harder to keep goals and objectives when we have shared them with others. Coaching is effective because you have made a promise to someone other than yourself–a public or social contract. This increases the execution factor because of the expected accountability.

Business coaching leads you to discover solutions and potential as well as possible obstacles to your organizations success. A coach is an expert on process and motivation, and simply guides you in the creation of your own plan of action.

We believe and have seen that people are fundamentally creative and resourceful; our job as coach is to show you how to tap into that creativity and those resources. You can expect great results from your Business Coaching relationship.

From the Coach:

"The great thing about the future is that it comes only one day at a time." - Abraham Lincoln ... We get to choose how we spend it.

Ask Yourself:

Who am I accountable to?

But encourage one another daily, as long as it is called "Today," so that none of you may be hardened by sin's deceitfulness. - Hebrews 3:13

Becoming an Outstanding Leader

Dear Coach,

I was just promoted to a leadership position within my department and I want to deliver positive results from the start. How can I be an effective leader with limited leadership background?
–New Leader

Dear New Leader,

Congratulations on your new role. The very term leader suggests that a person has the ability to gain followers. It has been said that a person marching ahead with no one behind isn't leading they are just taking a walk. Becoming a great leader requires us to develop character, people skills and apply timeless principles to our daily life. Having followers means more than a title or position. A leader is someone who has been able to influence others and convince them to go in a specific direction.

Peter Drucker, writer, management consultant and university professor, said, "Management is doing things right. Leadership is doing the right things."

Great leaders are capable of influencing others, while doing the right things. They do this by communicating purpose and vision to their staff while equipping the team to make informed, accountable decisions. Their focus is to execute the company's overall objectives and maximize the production, skills and talents of those they lead.

Franklin Covey conducted a private survey and asked 200,000 employees if their manager asks their opinion on how to do things better. The results showed 38 percent of employees said yes. A good way to frame leadership is realize that "We is better than Me." People will work harder if they are included in the way the work gets done.

Vision:
A good leader sees and thinks in future terms with a clear vision of a desire result. They also have foresight to see the speed bumps down the road. With proper communication, thorough planning, thoughtful managing, and a process of accountability, a company can thrive as far as the leader can see.

Communicate and Execute:
Leading to the final step is the ultimate goal, as well as recognizing them when you feel that you have reached that goal. Communication and execution are the often the missing link in many organizations. The results of this polling question may seem shocking. "What percentage of the people in your organization would say they have clear, measureable goals," 9 % of 200,000 organizations polled said they have a clear, measurable goal; 14 percent said they stayed focused on the most important goals; 10 percent said yes their success measures are tracked accurately and openly; and 16 percent said teams plan together how to achieve their goals.

Evaluate:
Everyone likes to know where they stand in the grand scheme of things. A systematic approach to giving and receiving feedback will improve the clarity of expectations. It is essential to evaluate specific actions and behaviors that are in line with the organizations overall values, vision and desired results. And when you are actively trying to raise an employee to their highest potential, it is helpful to give

at least four times the amount of positive feedback to one direct criticism.

Encourage Those You Lead:
According to Johann Wolfgang von Goethe, "The way you see people is the way you treat them, and the way you treat them is what they become." There are three ways to get the best out of others, and the first is appreciation. Every time you thank another person, you increase their self-esteem and improve their self-image. The second way is to give them praise and approval. When people feel approved it gives them the energy to go to the next level. The third way to empower others is to listen and pay close attention when they talk. This will take your leadership influence to new heights of success.

Patience:
While many claim that great leaders are born, leadership is something that can be learned. It is a skill that requires patience when working with others to persuade them to perform at their best. Great leadership takes time, have patience with your followers and yourself as you become an outstanding leader.

From the Coach:

You must first lead yourself in excellence before anyone else will want to follow you. Your self image will be an instrument gauging your leadership effectiveness.

Ask Yourself:

How well do I lead myself?

What promises can I keep to myself to improve?

No discipline seems pleasant at the time, but painful. Later on, however, it produces a harvest of righteousness and peace for those who have been trained by it. - Hebrews 12:11

Blowing the Whistle on Strife in the Workplace

Dear Coach,
I have gone from leader to referee. Members of my staff are in constant battle with one another and with me. This is creating an unpleasant and stressful environment. I have tried to be patient, but I need solutions!
–Blowing the Whistle on Strife

Dear Blowing the Whistle on Strife,
Peace should be a top priority in the workplace. The ability to address and resolve conflict is essential to effectiveness, productivity and profit.

Studies reveal a staggering 25 percent of employee time is spent engaging in–or trying to resolve–conflict. When emotions are high, intellect is low.

The Three Sources of Conflict
There are three main sources that cause conflict in the workplace: Hurt, fear and frustration.

Hurt is the source of much contention. Hurt is most often caused by vague expectations or jealousy–which leads to anger, resentment and revenge. Workplace anger is costly in time, mistakes, stress, morale, performance and customer service, not to mention the physical consequences of the angry person.

Fear is **F**alse **E**vidence **A**ppearing **R**eal. There are more fears and phobias than letters in the alphabet. Fear of failure, fear of success and fear of public humiliation are great contributors to conflict. Frustration is like water just about to boil. Every person has priorities and expectations. For example, being on time may be important to you; if your staff arrives late you may become frustrated.

Responses to Conflict
People respond to conflict in three ways: Explosion, implosion or resolution.

Explosion occurs when pressure exists. Jefferson said, "If you are angry, count to 10, if you are really angry count to 100." When we explode, anger turns into danger.

Implosion is like buried toxic waste waiting to surface. We can pretend it doesn't exist, but in truth it is growing. This repressed conflict can manifest itself into bitterness and depression among other physical and psychological problems.

The Road to Resolution: Recall, Resolve and Forgive
Recall the words or situation to give you insight. What part did you play in the conflict exchange? Try to understand the position of the other party and be flexible.

Resolve it. "Anyone who loves his opinion more than his teammates will advance his opinions but set back the team." –John C. Maxwell. Success is relational. No problem can withstand strategic, solution-focused thinking.

Forgive. Make the move and ask to be forgiven. Is forgiveness easy? No. Forgiveness does not mean that we agree or that we approve. Forgiveness allows us to let go of the wrongs done so we can release the anger and resentment. Learning to forgive will not only improve your health, it will allow you to refocus on more important objectives.

The ability to work together in harmony and to resolve inevitable conflicts are indispensable skills to long-term success. However, many organizations are far from peaceful. Instead they are faced with conflict, escalated tension and continual frustration. They are not working together for a common goal; they are in competition with each other.

As a leader you may consider communicating the purpose of each position as it relates to your corporate objective. This will create confidence and understanding. Develop a plan, processes or guidelines to deal with conflict. This will save time and resources when conflicts arise. Ask for input from your staff.

Depending on how we approach conflict, it can either stop us or stretch us so we not only overcome but we also become a better person in the process. It is our choice.

Conflicts, tension and challenges will always arise within the workplace, but we can learn how to deal effectively with them. This will prevent the eroding of trust and combat revenge. As we understand the root of many conflicts to be hurt, fear and frustration then we can see the solution in a more human light.

"Don't find fault; find a remedy." –Henry Ford

From the Coach:

There will always be opportunities to get upset, there will always be circumstances that are completely unfair and adversity that is beyond your control but you will FOREVER have the freedom to choose your responds to any situation.

Ask Yourself:

How can I create a more peaceful environment at work and home?

> Let the message of Christ dwell among you richly as you
> teach and admonish one another with all wisdom through
> psalms, hymns, and songs from the Spirit, singing to God
> with gratitude in your hearts. - Colossians 3:16

Coping with Stress

Dear Coach,
Our organization is going through change which is causing unbearable stress. Everyone is uptight. I am concerned about the effects of stress on our team, individually and our future success. What do you suggest?
–Not Coping with Stress

Dear Not Coping with Stress,
Even the news can bring on feelings of fear and uncertainty with reports of homes in foreclosure, bankrupt businesses and government spending out of control. Often when we focus on negative reports our stress is compounded. Here are some practical solutions for coping with stress.

Know What Stress Is and Its Effects
In 1956, McGraw-Hill released Dr. Hans Selye's book entitled The Stress of Life. It was based on his pioneering and revolutionary concepts of stress and its effects on us. Dr. Selye, often called, the father of the stress theory, defined stress as "the nonspecific response of the body to any demand made upon it." The "demand" can be a threat, a challenge or any kind of change which requires us to adapt. This reaction results from an outpouring of adrenaline and other

hormones that causes your blood pressure to increase, your heart to beat faster and your lungs to take in more air. Stress hormones actually give you extra strength and mental acuity for a few moments. These changes in the body are intended to be a natural defense called the "fight-or-flight response". Some stress is healthy and helps us perform at higher levels, but when the stress response occurs too frequently or goes on consistently over time, those hormones that were meant to save your life begin to destroy your health. They can lead to headaches, depression, anxiety, obesity, type 2 diabetes, hypertension and all kinds of illnesses. He causes of stress though many can be classified in two general groups: situations we can control and those that are uncontrollable or beyond our skill or knowledge. What we can control is our response to the circumstance. By practicing these stress- reducing habits we can lower the adverse effects of stress on ourselves and our organizations.

Mindfulness

Mindfulness is the practice of paying attention to what is going on moment to moment. It is slowing down, focusing on one activity at a time and enjoying the present moment. The inverse would be attending a staff meeting and your thoughts are focused on the tasks that await you after. It is difficult to relax and listen when you are anxious or thinking about the future, by not practicing mindfulness you could miss critical information.

Gratitude

Practice an "attitude of gratitude." There is a peacefulness that comes when we stop and give thanks. I suggest creating a list identifying at least twenty specific things, great and small for which you are grateful. Make your list a part of your mental dialogue every day.

Reframing

Reframing is taking thoughts; past, present or future, challenging them and choosing to see them from a fresh perspective. A powerful example of reframing is the story of Viktor Frankl, a Jewish psychiatrist and Holocaust survivor. Dr. Frankl's circumstances looked dismal but he knew the power within him. He had a freedom that even the Nazi captors could not take from him. This freedom was his power to choose his response. Like Frankl, we have the power to reframe and to see on the other side of the circumstances and envision the positive.

Humor

Create a habit of humor instead of worry. Worry is paying for something you may never get. Studies prove laughter boosts your immune system and lowers the levels of stress hormones. A merry heart is a great weapon against stress.

Margin

A wise way to de-stress is to build in margin. Margin is the buffer between panic and peace. When we fail to schedule adequate time between meetings, activities or events, we set ourselves up to experience stress. Building margin in your schedule, your finances, and other areas will prevent unnecessary stress.

Time-Outs

No one would expect an athlete to play an entire game without taking a break, yet statistics show that the average American is working an additional three hours per week compared with 20 years ago. That translates into an extra month per year. One of the first symptoms of distress is fatigue, which we tend to ignore. By taking quick time-outs during the day we can avoid exhaustion.

There are many other ways to cope with the daily stresses of this world, like getting plenty of sleep, maintaining a healthy diet, drinking filtered water, reducing caffeine, regular exercise, meditation, music, breathing and taking a vacation. I consider one of the greatest ways to reduce your stress level is to take the focus off your own circumstances and go fulfill a need for someone else. It puts things into perspective.

From the Coach:

Things can be worst in our mind than they are in reality. Discouragement is a tactic from the opposition to keep you where you are... Don't fall prey and believe the lie. Believe you can!

Ask Yourself:

What dominates my thoughts?

How can I take a break and reduce my stress?

So now I am giving you a new commandment: Love each other. Just as I have loved you, you should love each other. Your love for one another will prove to the world that you are my disciples. – John 13:35-35 NLT

Love is Patient

Dear Coach,
There are a few co-workers that have some extreme personalities and lifestyles that I am finding very hard to deal with. I know that I am supposed to love them as Christ loves me but sometimes I'm not sure how much more I can take.
–Help Me Love More

Dear Help Me Love More,
In times of extreme demand or critical deadlines people can seem impatient and short tempered. While most of us don't have to deal with life or death dilemmas or daring rescues, we all have opportunities to keep calm, walk in love and extend patience under pressure and adversity.

Our everyday activities and interaction with other people deplete our physical and spiritual energy. In fact every non-spiritual activity is burning up spiritual fuel. The secret to a loving and patient lifestyle can be found here in Jude. Jude 1:20 tells us, "But you, beloved, build yourself up founded on your most holy faith, make progress, rise like an edifice (structure) higher and higher, praying in the Holy Spirit; Guard and keep yourself in the love of God; expecting and patiently waiting for the mercy of our Lord Jesus Christ, the Messiah which will bring you into eternal life." He said to guard and keep ourselves in the Love of God.

In 1 Corinthians 13:4-8, love's character is described as patient. According to Webster's, patience is bearing pains or trials calmly and without complaint. Patience is steadfast despite opposition, difficulty or adversity. The lack of patience is easy to see and often demonstrated when plans don't go according to our expectations. People think patience is something you just have but rather it is a decision you make. That is why patience is misunderstood, sometimes hard to implement and even harder to maintain. Interestingly, we can't practice being patient without being in a situation that requires it. As we grow to new levels, we understand and accept that not everyone is going to do everything exactly the way we think it should be done nor as fast as we think it should be done.

Be encouraged today, walking in the Love of God or Agape Love and being patient is a decision to be obedient to God, not a feeling or natural immediate responds. Many times we have to hold our tongue until our spirit overrides our flesh. Proverbs 15:1 says, "A soft answer turns away wrath, but grievous words stir up anger." It takes patience to restrain our flesh. Our flesh wants to sir it up, pick a fight, throw a tantrum and have everything our way. But God's ways are higher than our ways. God's love has been poured out in our hearts by His Holy Spirit. That outpouring produces the fruit of the Spirit and the character of God. People are not perfect but God's love is, and love is patient.

From the Coach:

Love can be translated to the behavior it produces. When we love someone we treat them with honor and respect. We would never intentionally hurt, or gossip about, or betray someone we love. Love is a choice not a feeling. And if we are Disciples of Christ then to love is required.

Ask Yourself:

How do I demonstrate God's love to those around me?

Am I truly aware of how much God loves me?

Now faith is the confidence in what we hope for and assurance about what we do not see. – Hebrews 11:1

Uncompromising Faith

Dear Coach,
I am afraid I will get caught up in the world's way of thinking, what can I do to stay true to what I believe? – Living in the System

Dear Living in the System,
David said in Psalms 37:25, "I was young and now I am old, yet I have never seen the righteous forsaken or their children begging for bread."

The world calls the ways of God foolish. To stay faithful to God we must create habits to keep our mind renewed. Those habits include devotion to His word, praise and worship, being thankful and keeping like-minded company. We have to be careful what we allow ourselves to be exposed to. If the lifestyle of the world becomes familiar we can over time rationalize behavior as normal or accepted. In the face of the uncertainty of the world, you will build your faith by dwelling on the Word of God. When you do, something will change on the inside of you. A confidence in God will stir up and unleash a powerful, unstoppable force. David possessed that unstoppable force because of his uncompromising faith in God. Nothing could change his belief in God's faithful and loving nature. No matter what David faced he was certain he would not face it alone.

In 1 Samuel 1:17:45, "David said to the Philistine, 'You come against me with sword and spear and javelin, but I come against you in the name of the Lord Almighty, the God of the armies of Israel, whom you have defiled. This day the Lord will hand you over to me, and I will strike you down.'" David did not run at Goliath with his mouth shut. He spoke to the giant and told him exactly what was going to happen, before he ever threw the first stone.

The determining factor in what you have is not what others say, but what you say. Jesus taught us in Mark 11:23 that if we would speak to our mountain and not doubt in our heart, the mountain would be removed. Imagine what is on the other side of your mountain. David knew on the other side of defeating Goliath was honor, wealth and favor. But greater than all these, the people gathered there would know that it is not by sword or spear but the Lord that is mighty to save.

Be encouraged today; whatever "Giant" you may be facing know that God is with you. When we have uncompromising faith in God and in the promises of His Word, our faith will cause us to win in any circumstance. Smith Wigglesworth said, "I am not moved by what I see. I am moved only by what I believe. I know this, no man looks at appearances if he believes. No man considers how he feels if he believes. The man, who believes God, HAS IT."

From the Coach:

To stay faithful to the ways of God we must create habits to keep our mind renewed. Those habits include devotion to God's word, praise, worship, thanksgiving and keeping like-minded company. We have to be careful what we allow ourselves to be exposed to. If the lifestyle of the world becomes familiar we can over time rationalize behavior as normal or accepted.

Ask Yourself:

Am I staying true to what I believe or Am I being persuaded to think like the crowd?

What habits do I need to create to stay on course with God?

Consider it all JOY, when you encounter various trials... knowing that the testing of your faith produces endurance. – James 1:2-3

Living UP in a Down World

Dear Coach,
When my day starts I am excited about what is to come but by the time I arrive at my place of employment, I feel like I have had all the life drained out of me. I pray constantly but I still feel like nothing is going right. How can I live a more excited life?
–Needs More Joy

Dear Needs More Joy,
Are you frustrated with circumstances in life? Do you seem tired, anxious or depressed when you think about the condition of our world?

The truth is we all face times of challenge but there is a way to maintain a good outlook and be "UP" in a down world. Knowing Jesus Christ as Lord and understanding what He has provided in His redemptive work gives us the freedom to follow His Word and be UP in a down world.

These four fundamental attitudes are the essentials to living UP in a down world.

1. Thanksgiving
2. Praise
3. Obedience
4. Submission

Thanksgiving

Often times we get so problem minded that we forget to thank God for what He has done in our life. Philippians 4:6 says, "Be careful for nothing; but in everything by prayer and supplication with thanksgiving let your requests be made known unto God." Everything in your life may not be exactly the way you want it to be but be encouraged it is changeable. Thanksgiving is fundamental to refocus our thinking and attention to what is good in our life. We can be thankful in all things. We thank God for our salvation. Thank God, He has redeemed us from the curse of the law. Thank God, He is our healer and our deliverer. Thank God, He has translated us out of darkness into the Kingdom of His dear Son. Thanks be to God who gives us the victory through Jesus Christ.

Praise

Isaiah 61:3 says, "To appoint unto them that mourn in Zion, to give unto them beauty for ashes, the oil of joy for mourning, the **garment** of **praise** for the spirit of heaviness; that they might be called trees of righteousness, the planting of the LORD, that he might be glorified." Praise is not a feeling but an attitude of love toward our Heavenly Father. We don't have to put up with depressing feelings or thoughts, we can praise God. Our garment of praise is a weapon that defeats the spirit of heaviness. Praise You, God!

Obedience

Romans 6:16 says, "Know you not, that to whom you yield yourselves servants to obey, his servants you are to whom you obey; whether of sin unto death, or of **obedience** unto righteousness?" Obedience comes from the Greek word–Hupakoe which means to hear. We can't be obedient to God unless we hear what He is saying. There is a difference between being a pupil and a disciple. A pupil is someone who receives information or hears the word. While a disciple is a person who hears God's Word and puts into practice what was heard. Obedience is connected to our faith and real faith translates into action.

Submission

James 4:7-8, "Submit yourselves therefore to God. Resist the devil, and he will flee from you. Draw nigh to God, and he will draw nigh to you." If thanksgiving, praise, obedience and submission to God are a daily act and habit in your life then there is a resistance to the devil on the inside of you. There is a resistance to the force of darkness and to the attacks that the enemy may bring against your life.

Be encouraged today, when we have these four fundamentals attitudes of thanksgiving, praise, obedience and submission to God at work in our lives then we have the devil backed in a corner. He has no weapon that can defeat us or keep us down. In Christ, we live UP in a down world.

From the Coach:

There is a time for everything, and a season for every activity under heaven. - Ecclesiastes 3:1 God has an awesome plan for your life. The secret to peace is understanding and trusting in God's perfect timing.

Ask Yourself:

What are at least ten things that I am thankful for?

How can I remind myself that true submission to God is to live with thanksgiving and praise regardless of the circumstances?

If anyone will not welcome you or listen to your words, leave that home or town and shake the dust off your feet. – Matthew 10:14

Shake It Off

Dear Coach,
Do you believe everyone has to go through adversity? – Why Me

Dear Why Me,
I believe to stand in the place God calls you to, yes you will have times of testing and proving your faith. Throughout the Apostle Paul's life he traveled tremendous distances and experienced many suspenseful events. After his transformation from persecutor of Christians to preacher for Christ, it was estimated that he covered more than 13,000 miles. During his travels things didn't always go according to what he planned or expected. At times it looked more like a legal journey than a missionary journey as he faced opposition with governors, kings, religious and other prominent leaders.

In Acts 28:1, we find Paul and 276 other soldiers and prisoners safely on the shores of Malta. After a violent storm, their ship had struck a sandbar and ran aground. The bow stuck fast and would not move, and the stern was broken to pieces by the pounding surf. Once on the island, the natives showed them unusual kindness. Due to the cold and rain, the natives built a fire as they welcomed them all. Paul gathered a pile of brushwood and as he put it on the fire, a viper, driven out by the heat, fastened itself on his hand. When the islanders saw the snake hanging from his hand, they said to each other, "This man must be a murderer; for though he escaped from the sea, Justice has not allowed him to live."

Can you imagine being in Paul's position? It seemed like Paul was dealing with one thing after another. The natives of Malta reminding him of his past mistakes saying he must be a murderer. He had refuted accusations from lawyers and religious leaders in Caesarea; he had overcome standing before King Agrippa, survived a violent storm and a shipwreck. Now he's been bitten by a viper and the report is he is going to die.

Like Paul, we have encountered times of challenge. Maybe you have been challenged with a report that sounds discouraging or you may have heard the enemy tried to remind you of your past mistakes and make you question who you are. It is not the event, but how we respond to what happens that develops us. When we respond with what God's Word says, we will always win.

In verse 5 we see Paul's responds, "But Paul shook the snake off into the fire and suffered no ill effects." Paul took God at His Word and shook it off. God had promised Paul that he would live and not die, that He would rescue him from his own people. God told Paul that he was forgiven and cleansed from all unrighteousness. Because of Jesus, Paul was **saved** (Acts 16:30-33), **a new creature** (2 Cor. 5-7), **a son of God** (1 Jn. 3:1-2), **joint heir with Christ** (Rm. 8:16-17), **healed** (1 Peter 2:24), **protected** (Ps. 91), **redeemed from the curse of spiritual death, poverty and sickness** (Gal.3:13) **loved** (Eph. 2:4-5) **eternally alive** (Rm.6:23), **highly favored** (Ps.5:12) **and had authority on earth and over the devil** (Eph.2:6).

God's Word is truth and God's promises are for anyone who will believe. God promises us in His Word when we keep our mind focused on Him then He will keep us in perfect peace.

Paul took God at His Word and used every circumstance to further advance the mission that God had called him to complete. Through his series of legal trials and transactions Paul was eventually delivered to Rome where his presentation of the gospel would penetrate even into the walls of the emperor's palace.

Be encouraged today, no matter where you are; God has equipped you with the power to "Shake It Off." As we worship, honor and magnify God, everything we are going through will come into right perspective. Take God at His Word and say what He says.

From the Coach:

You are who God says you are… Resist entertaining the negative identity that the enemy wants you to embrace. You are an overcomer!

Ask Yourself:

What does God say about me?

What does He say about my future? Jeremiah 29:11

Whose report am I going to believe?

Many are the plans in a person's heart; but it is the LORD'S purpose that prevails. - Proverbs 19:21

How Great is Our God!

Dear Coach,
What should I do when I feel like giving up? – Growing Tired

Dear Growing Tired
David wrote in Psalms 34:1-4, "I will bless the Lord at all times; His praise shall continually be in my mouth. My life makes its boast in the Lord; let the humble and afflicted hear and be glad. O magnify the Lord with me, and let us exalt His name together. I sought (inquired of) the Lord and required Him [of necessity and on the authority of His Word], and He heard me, and delivered me from all my fears."

When you look at things through a magnifying glass the object is enlarged. The same is true when we focus on or continually talk about negative circumstances. Instead of magnifying the problem we should magnify God and His greatness. God pays attention when His people call on Him. David cried out not in despair but in praise. David was magnifying the greatness of God during a very difficult time in his life. He had experienced success through the delivering power of God but when he wrote Psalm 34, his life was far from perfect. David didn't write this psalm of praise from the mountain top. He had been on the run and just escaped near death from Achish, King of Gath.

God is bigger than any circumstances we face and He is able to deliver us from all our fears. Whether God shows us a way of escape or strengthens us in times of troubles, we can be certain that He always hears and responds to those who love and fear Him.

David went on to say in verse 6-9, "This poor man cried, and the Lord heard him, and saved him out of all his troubles. The Angel of the Lord encamps around those who fear Him [who revere and worship Him with awe] and each of them He delivers. O taste and see that the Lord [our God] is good! Blessed (happy, fortunate, to be envied) is the man who trusts and takes refuge in Him. O fear the Lord, you His saints [revere and worship Him]! For there is no want to those who truly revere and worship Him with godly fear."

Be encouraged today, God knows not some things, but all things. He has the answers to all of life's questions. He knows the end at the beginning and every step in between. When we magnify God, worship, reverence and trust in Him we will see His hand upon our lives. He promises great blessings to His people and He directs our steps into a peaceful and abundant life. Those promises require our active participation through faith.

From the Coach:

Fear sees what man sees; Faith sees what God sees. Fear creates paralysis while Faith creates action.

Ask Yourself:

What are my greatest fears?

What would I attempt if I knew I would not fail?

Jesus answered, "I am the way and the truth and the life. No one comes to the Father except through Me." —John 14:6

· ·

The Way

Dear Coach,
I am looking for the right path for my life. How can I find purpose? –
Seeking the Meaning

Dear Seeking the Meaning,
For centuries people from every corner of the world have searched for the way. The quest for purpose and fulfillment has consumed the minds and hearts of even the greatest leaders. There is something deep within us that longs to make a mark on the world, but when left alone we tend to lose our way. God created us for a divine purpose and to live with Him for all eternity. God also created the desire for significance within us. God loves us so much that He did not leave us alone to stumble upon our destiny, or for us to get "good enough" to get into the kingdom of heaven. God made "**The Way.**"

There are a number of people claiming to know the way to a happier, healthier, more successful you. Some have books about how to live in peace and how to get to heaven. Some promise a quick fix to all your problems, some claim there's a secret formula, while others believe through personal goodness that you can be granted access. Deuteronomy 8:16-18

who fed you in the wilderness with manna that your fathers did not know, that He might humble you and test you, to do you good in the end. Beware lest you say in your heart, 'My power and the might of my hand have gotten me this wealth.' You shall remember the LORD your GOD, for it is He who gives you power to get wealth, that He may confirm His covenant that He swore to your fathers, as it is this day.

In John 14:4-6 Jesus told his disciples, "You know the way to the place where I am going?" Thomas pleaded with Jesus and said, "Lord, we do not know where You are going, so how can we know the way?" Jesus answered, "I am the Way, and the Truth and the Life. No one comes to the Father except through me."

Jesus did not say I am **a** Way; He said "I am **the** Way." Do you need direction in your life? Is there an area you can't cope with alone? Jesus is **The Way.** Your situation may seem impossible but with God all things are possible. When you know Jesus, you know **The Way.** Jesus knows every challenge what you are facing and He knows the Way. Jesus is the Way to salvation; Jesus is the Way to healing. Jesus is the Way to restoring that relationship, Jesus is the Way out of that addiction; Jesus is the Way, and the Truth and the Life. Call on the matchless name of Jesus, in Him is everything. Be encouraged today, Jesus is the Way. Because of Jesus we can come boldly to the Father and receive all that He has promised.

From the Coach:

Today millions of people are in pursuit of a better life, a life of peace and happiness. The truth is there is only one way to the abundant life we have dreamed of here on earth and only one way to access God Himself. The Way is Jesus.

Ask Yourself:

Am I looking for people to share the saving truth of the Gospel of Jesus?

Do not conform to the pattern of this world, but be transformed by the renewing of your mind. Then you will be able to test and approve what God's will is —his good, pleasing and perfect will. - Romans 12:2

Blessing Explosion

Dear Coach,
What can I do to transform my current circumstances? – Less than Favorable

Dear Less than Favorable,
In the early development of major interstates, engineers would use dynamite explosions to remove obstacles and even mountains that stood in the way of the predetermined path. These explosions would transform the natural landscape. The word "explosion" in Merriam-Webster is defined as a large-scale, rapid and spectacular expansion, bursting out or forth.

Imagine a large-scale, rapid and spectacular burst of God's power and blessing in your life. Visualize what a "Blessing Explosion" could do to transform the landscape of your circumstances.

Paul and Silas experienced circumstances that looked less than favorable. Acts 16:16-38 describes Paul and Silas in real trouble. After commanding an evil spirit to come out of a fortune-telling girl, Paul and Silas were seized and dragged before the magistrates. Her owners realized that their hope of making money was gone. Along with the girl's owners, the crowd joined in the attack against them.

Paul and Silas were stripped, beaten, flogged and thrown into prison. But not just any cell, they were put in the inner cell and their feet fastened with stocks. Stocks were made of two boards joined with iron clamps leaving holes just big enough for the ankles. Paul and Silas had committed no crime but were being held as the most dangerous prisoners in absolute security.

Verse 25 says, "About midnight Paul and Silas were praying and singing praise to God, and the other prisoners were listening to them." They had just been beaten and flogged, yet they were not crying or complaining, they were praying and singing. They were magnifying God. What happens when we focus on God? Verse 26 tells us, "Suddenly there was such a violent earthquake that the foundations of the prison were shaken. At once all the prison doors flew open, and everybody's chains came loose."

Paul and Silas trusted God enough to know that God would make a way. God would not leave them stranded or helpless. God was at work while Paul and Silas were praying and praising. This blessing explosion delivered great results. Paul and Silas were freed and the jailer and his household, astonished by the miraculous events, received Jesus as their Lord and Savior. They were baptized and their lives changed forever.

Be encouraged today, God is never taken by surprise by your situation. He is the Alpha and Omega. He knows your future better than you know your past. God knows the end at the beginning and His plans lead to a great future. His "Blessing Explosion" is at work right now removing every obstacle and mountain that stands in your road to success.

Tammy Holyfield

From the Coach:

By trusting God and focusing on Him and His limitless power, we can transform our atmosphere.

Ask Yourself:

Do I pray and praise or worry and pace?

Who is greater and has the power to create change in my life?

Publish his glorious deeds among the nations. Tell everyone about the amazing things he does. – Psalm 96:3

Publish His Mercy to the Whole World

Dear Coach,
How can I make everything count? – Want to Make a Difference

Dear Want to Make a Difference,
Have you ever considered your life to be a published work? What if all your thoughts, conversations and actions were published for the whole world? Would the ways of God, His mercy, love and kindness be in print? In fact, we encounter many people as we navigate through our day. We must be aware that every moment someone is reading the pages of our life.

As Christians, we should live a life worthy of our call. Our lifestyle is evangelism as we reach out to shine our light in a dark world. At home, at school, at church and in business, we are called to consistently exhibit the character of God. In 1 Peter 3:15, Peter said, "But in your hearts set apart Christ as Lord. Always be prepared to give an answer to everyone who asks you to give a reason for the hope that you have. But do this with gentleness and respect." As people see the hope, joy and blessing in your life they will want to know your secret. In Acts 1:8 Jesus said, "But you will receive power when the Holy Spirit comes on you; and you will be my witness in Jerusalem, and in all Judea and Samaria, and to the ends of the earth.

There are over seven billion people who inhabit this earth. And of those there is an estimated 5.5 billion who don't know Jesus as Lord and Savior. The shocking news is that only about 4% of our youngest generation here in America professes Jesus as Lord. And even more disturbing, every 22 seconds someone dies? These facts are like an alarm going off in our hearts saying, "Wake up and see the reality of eternity." There is a heaven to gain and somewhere someone is waiting to hear the "Good News". Someone needs to know that God is good. Someone needs to hear that God loves you and He has an awesome plan for your life. People think that they have been too bad or are unworthy of God's love. But the truth is you can't get bad enough for God to turn away from you and you can't get good enough to get to God. God made the way for us to be reconciled to Him. Jesus is the "Good News". When you receive Jesus as your Lord and Savior, He makes you a new creation. Your past sins are not only forgiven, but forgotten. You are cleansed and restored back into right standing with God. We can run to God not from Him. That is awesome news. Be encouraged today, it is the goodness of God that draws people to repentance. Trust in God, He will cause people to cross your path who need Jesus. Be willing to share the amazing work that God has done in your life and publish His mercy to the whole world.

Three Ways to Win Your World for Jesus

1. **Live it.** Be a living example of Jesus, His ways of mercy, love and kindness. We can ruin our testimony by a harsh word spoken or dealing with someone in a rude or selfish matter. People are watching us, show them Jesus.
2. **Share the Word.** God's Word is truth, let the Word speak. Romans 3:23 says, "For all have sinned and fall short of the glory of God." Romans 6:23 says, "For the wages of sin is death, but the gift of God is eternal life in Christ Jesus our Lord." and Romans 10:13 says, "For whosoever shall call upon the Name of the Lord shall be saved."

3. **Prove it.** People may not know what you were like before you meet Jesus. Sharing your transformation will give hope to others. The Word of God says that we overcome by the blood of the lamb and the word of our testimony.

From the Coach:

Leaders LEAD! Don't be subject to the environment. Create it! You set the standard, atmosphere and end result. Someone is watching your example.

Ask Yourself:

What would the world look like if the whole world was filled with people just like me?

He Gives You Power!

Dear Coach,
How can I make more money? – $$$

Dear $$$
When we think of making more money we may think of our list of contacts or ways to become famous, like producing that social media post or video that goes viral, maybe start our own business or the latest get rich quick program.

Have you ever wondered what it would be like to be endorsed? Think of celebrities and athletes, they get paid millions of dollars each year by sponsors for the "right to use their name". They get special favor and star treatment wherever they go. It's because their gifts and talents have been "endorsed". The same is true for us. Just think when you receive Jesus as Lord and Savior, you get God's endorsement. When God's endorsement is upon your life, you get the rights to "His Name"!!!

Deuteronomy 8:16-18 who fed you in the wilderness with manna that your fathers did not know, that He might humble you and test you, to do you good in the end. Beware lest you say in your heart, 'My power and the might of my hand have gotten me this wealth.' You shall remember the LORD your GOD, for it is He who gives you power to get wealth, that He may confirm His covenant that

He swore to your fathers, as it is this day. Wealth is simply having abundance. God wants you to live in abundance so that He can use you to be a blessing to others. He gives us His power to prosper to establish His covenant on this earth and to promote the gospel of Jesus Christ. When we are willing and obedient to Him, we open the door to His promises. In other words, when we live in excellence and integrity, when we follow the standards of His Word, we will walk in His favor and blessing.

Notice it says that "He gives us the power to get wealth." God doesn't rain money down from Heaven. God gives ability and wisdom. He gives creative ideas, inventions, innovations, divine connections and relationships. We have to be diligent, do our part and step out to use what He's given us. Be encouraged today, by receiving His power and choosing a life of integrity we can move forward into the abundant life He has prepared for us.

From the Coach:

Today millions of people are in pursuit of a better life, a life of peace and happiness. The truth is there's only one way to the abundant life we have dreamed of here on earth and only one way to access God Himself. The Way is Jesus.

Ask Yourself:

Do I see God as my source?

I sought the LORD and asked what else can I do? Is there something more that You require of me? He answered saying, "Do what is right, Love mercy and walk humbly with Me." ~ paraphrased Micah 6:8

Come Unto Me

Dear Coach,

I need a break a place to rest, any ideas? – Burnt Out

Dear Burnt Out,

We are often unaware of our behavior when you are tired or under extreme pressure. When we get to that point, words like short, easily offended, insensitive, intense or impatience can describe us. Sometimes we resemble a well shaken soda can ready to explode. But did you know that God wants to give you rest? He wants to refresh and restore your mind, will and emotions as well as your physical body.

Life happens fast and it is easy to get caught up in the burden of busyness. We were created to grow, achieve and succeed. But when we are extremely busy, stressed or worried, our mind, will and emotions can get so carbonated that we can't think straight. The enemy tries to convince us we are too busy and have too many other responsibilities to spend quality time with God. The truth is most of the time we are busier in our minds than we are physically.

In Matthew 11:28-30, Jesus said, "Come to me, all you who are weary and burdened, and I will give you rest. Take my yoke upon you and learn from me, for I am gentle and humble in heart, and you will find rest for your souls. For my yoke is easy and my burden is light."

When we pause and come into God's presence, He neutralizes our life. Being with God helps us to get the right perspective and align our priorities. I have found spending time with God will actually help you get more done in less time. But even among the hustle of life, we can find rest, refreshing and relaxation. God wants us to enjoy life. That's why He said to come to Him. The more we know God, the more we trust Him to take care of everything that concerns us. Be encouraged today, the key to experiencing this rest in your life everyday is to everyday consistently "Come unto Him". Release your cares to the Lord, you will find rest and live the abundant life that He promised.

From the Coach:

There will always be that moment in the JOURNEY when you aren't sure if you have what it takes to finish... But you have come too far to quit. HOPE will say have the courage to BELIEVE one more day. Your finishing strong will rest in knowing what's at stake.

Ask Yourself:

Do I feel guilt when I rest? WHY?

* *

The Secret Place

Dear Coach,
I need a place of escape. What do you suggest? - OVERWHELMED

Dear OVERWHELMED,
Are you facing a seemingly impossible challenge or situation? It may have fell as if the whole world was crashing in around you. Something inside cried out for peace in the midst of calamity or maybe you longed to get away to a safe and quiet place of refuge.

There is a place where you can experience a shift. A place where stress and anxiety melt away and fear is replaced by faith and trust in God.

Where is this place? Psalm 91, tells us of the secret place of the Most High. The secret place is where God reassures you He is in control and on your side. It's the place where God encourages and strengthens you by His Spirit.

Psalm 91 says, "He who dwells in the secret place of the Most High shall remain stable and fixed under the shadow of the Almighty whose power no foe can withstand. When we dwell in the secret place then we will say, God is my Refuge and my Fortress, my God; on Him I lean and rely, and in Him I confidently trust! The more you know God the more you will trust Him in every area of your life. The safest place in the world to be is in the Will of God.

Psalms 91:3-16, goes on to promise, "For [then] He will deliver you from the snare of the fowler and from the deadly pestilence. Then He will cover you with His opinions, and under His wings shall you trust and find refuge; His truth and His faithfulness are a shield and a buckler. You shall not be afraid of the terror of the night, nor of the arrow (the evil plots and slanders of the wicked) that flies by day, Nor of the pestilence that stalks in darkness, nor of the destruction and sudden death that surprise and lay waste at noonday. A thousand may fall at your side, and ten thousand at your right hand, but it shall not come near you. Only a spectator shall you be [yourself inaccessible in the secret place of the Most High] as you witness the reward of the wicked. Because you have made the Lord your refuge, and the Most High your dwelling place, there shall no evil befall you, nor any plague or calamity come near your tent. For He will give His angels charge over you to accompany and defend and preserve you in all your ways of obedience and service. They shall bear you up on their hands, lest you dash your foot against a stone. You shall tread upon the lion and adder; the young lion and the serpent shall you trample underfoot."

Verse 16, "Because he has set his love upon Me," says the Lord, "I will deliver him; I will set him on high, because he knows and understands My name has a personal knowledge of My mercy, love, and kindness—trusts and relies on Me, knowing I will never forsake him, no, never. He shall call upon Me, and I will answer him; I will be with him in trouble, I will deliver him and honor him. With long life will I satisfy him and show him My salvation."

Be encouraged today, God is a shelter and a refuge from all of the demands of life. When we dwell in His "Secret Place" our emotions will neutralize as peace and clarity spring forth. Our trust in Almighty God as our protector and deliverer will carry us through to the place of freedom and victory.

Tammy Holyfield

From the Coach:

Believing the promises in God's word is a place of peace and safety.

Ask Yourself:

When the demands of life overwhelm me where do I turn to escape?

*"As I was with Moses, so I will be with you; I will
never leave you or forsake you." – Joshua 1:5*

The Lifestyle of Faith

Dear Coach,
I want to be a better leader, where should I begin? – Room for
Improvement

Dear Room for Improvement,
Leadership is about a lifestyle of faith. Joshua lived a great example
of someone who truly understood the lifestyle of faith. He had
experienced amazing displays of God's supernatural power as well
as disappointment, defeat and great adversity. After Moses died,
Joshua was one of only two people alive who had seen firsthand the
Egyptian plagues and the exodus from Egypt. God entrusted Joshua
to lead the people of Israel into the promise land. After wandering
for forty years in the desert, a new generation was ready to enter
Canaan. Before Joshua's great battle of Jericho, God spoke a promise,
instruction and encouragement to equip him for victory. In Joshua
1:5 God said to him, "As I was with Moses, so I will be with you;
I will never leave you or forsake you." God placed on the inside of
Joshua seeds of greatness; a big vision, a hope and a dream. Joshua
had a choice, to be a man of great and unwavering faith or to coward
down and disappoint God.

Can you imagine getting a big promotion and then finding out
that one of your job responsibilities was to bring down a military
superpower? The Canaanites considered the Wall of Jericho to be

invincible but God told Joshua that Jericho was already delivered into his hands. God gave him specific instructions to win the battle. Envision being told that if you march around once a day for six days a wall that was built thousands of years before you were born, twenty five feet high and twenty feet thick. Then on the seventh day march seven times, sound a trumpet and tell all the people to give a loud shout. After the shout then the wall will collapse. That is mind boggling. In our natural way of thinking that sounds impossible. Joshua may have thought, this is too complicated, I am not qualified; this is over my head, what if I fail? He may not have been able to understand with his mind, but Joshua was bold enough to believe and do what God asked him to do. When God commissioned Joshua, he told him three times to be strong and courageous. God knew what Joshua needed to accomplish the goal. God even prepared Joshua with an action plan for success. In Joshua 1:8 God instructed him to meditate on His Word day and night and do all that is written in it.

Still today God has deposited seeds of greatness in each of us. We must let those seeds take root. You may have a dream right now, maybe it's a new career or relationship or maybe it's a dream of being completely healed. Don't let go of your faith, stand firm and immoveable, believing what God said. Faith begins where the will of God is known. Joshua knew God's will and he trusted God every step of the way. Hebrews 11:6 says, "Without faith it is impossible to please God." When God plants a dream in our heart, He will always equip us for success. Our job is to believe.

Living a lifestyle of faith requires us to focus on God and not our circumstances or what may seem like the impossible. When the God kind of faith rises up in you, there will always be opposition. Two voices competing for your attention; the voice of victory and the voice of defeat. In our heart we believe but often our reason will try to talk us out of it. Be encouraged today as you listen and follow the voice of victory. God is with you and He has equipped you to live the lifestyle of faith.

From the Coach:

A good leader inspires people to have confidence in their leader. A GREAT leader inspires people to have confidence in themselves.

Ask Yourself:

What is the VOICE of Defeat saying?

What is the VOICE of Victory saying?

Which ONE will I choice to believe?

> But when you ask, you must believe and not doubt,
> because the one who doubts is like a wave of the sea,
> blown and tossed by the wind. - James 1:6

Deciding to Believe God

Dear Coach,

Not sure who to believe anymore, what's the truth? – Doubting

Dear Doubting,

We have all been in a place where we didn't understand or we have found ourselves questioning God's will for our life? Or maybe wrestled with thoughts of unbelief? Often, I hear people question the promises of God based on how they feel. We all have feelings but feelings shouldn't determine our decisions. That mindset says if I feel depressed then I must be. The truth is our feelings and circumstances are constantly changing. Our feelings are emotions not reality. When we decide to believe God, His Word and His promises, it is not based on what we feel.

Romans 10:10 says, "For with the heart a person believes (adheres to, trusts in, and relies on Christ) and so is justified (declared righteous, acceptable to God), and with the mouth he confesses (declares openly and speaks out freely his faith) and confirms his salvation." We believe God with our heart, not our mind, our feelings or our emotions.

Notice Paul said when we believe in Jesus then we are justified, declared righteous and acceptable to God. Righteousness is not a state of development. When you confess your sins, repent and receive Jesus as Lord and Savior, you become right with God. Often, people have a hard time believing the promises of God apply to them because of their past failures. This is where the enemy tries to confuse God's people. Satan will take every opportunity to remind you of times you missed it or whisper lies of how unworthy you are to receive God's best. God wants you to see yourself through the redemptive work of Jesus. You are a child of the Most High and God's promises are Yes and Amen.

In verse 17 Paul says, "So faith comes by hearing [what is told], and what is heard comes by the preaching [of the message that came from the lips] of Christ (the Messiah Himself)." Our faith will grow and believe whatever we are hearing. That is why we must stay focused on God's Word.

Hebrews 11:1-6 says, "NOW FAITH is the assurance, the confirmation, the title deed of the things we hope for, being the proof of things we do not see and the conviction of their reality faith perceiving as real fact what is not revealed to the senses. For by faith trust and holy fervor born of faith the men of old had divine testimony borne to them and obtained a good report."

By faith we understand that the worlds during the successive ages were framed fashioned, put in order, and equipped for their intended purpose by the word of God, so that what we see was not made out of things which are visible.

Verse 6 says, "But without faith it is impossible to please and be satisfactory to Him. For whoever would come near to God must necessarily believe that God exists and that He is the rewarder of those who earnestly and diligently seek Him out."

Be encouraged today, believing God is a decision that pleases God. Habakkuk 2:4 tells us that the just or righteous shall live by faith.

Tammy Holyfield

Our faith is the hand that reaches into the realm of the Spirit to get all that God has. God is not a man that He should lie; if He said it you can believe it. He is the Great I AM, Creator of heaven and earth. Believe and receive all that He has promised you.

From the Coach:

We believe God with our heart, not our mind, our feelings or our emotions.

You'll forget all about your struggles when you are holding your promise.

Ask Yourself:

Do I deserve success?

Where does faith come from?

For I know the plans I have for you, declares the LORD,
plans to prosper you and not to harm you, plans to
give you hope and a future. – Jeremiah 29:11

I Know Who I Am

Dear Coach,
Sometimes I question my purpose. – Who am I

Dear Who am I,
There's within us a curiosity to uncover the secrets and mysteries of life. Who am I? And why am I here? Most people at some point in life's journey have pondered these questions. The answers can be traced back to our origin. In the beginning God created man from the dust of the ground; He fashioned the body and breathed the breath of life into him and he became a living soul. He became a speaking spirit. God made us in His image and in His likeness. We are created in the image of God, to follow the ways of God.

In the Garden of Eden, Adam made the mistake of believing a lie from Satan, as a result, we were separated from God, cut off from our source of life. Without God and a relationship with Him, there is a void in the human soul, one that longs for connection. That connection can only be completed when we come to the saving knowledge of Jesus Christ who reconnects us with our source of life, our creator, our Father, our identity.

Satan wants to steal your identity. The last thing he wants is for you to know who you are, your purpose and above all your authority as a believer in Jesus Christ. If Satan can convince you to see who you are in yourself then he can succeed in stealing your peace and stir up feelings of confusion, frustration, fear and worry.

How do you see yourself, through the eyes of your environment, situation or circumstance? God is calling you out to discover your true identity. He wants you to see a new vision for your life. God wants you to see yourself through His eyes, the eyes of love, truth and faith. If you desire to make your mark on the world then spend time with the One who created it.

In Genesis 13, God called Abram out and spoke this promise, "I will make you into a great nation and I will bless you; I will make your name great, and you will be a blessing. I will bless those who bless you, and whoever curses you I will curse; and all peoples on the earth will be blessed through you." Abram waited for 24 years to become all that God had told him he would be. During that time Abram was not perfect, he and Sarah, his wife attempted to assist God by forcing His plans into action. Then in Chapter 17, at the age of ninety-nine, the Lord appeared to Abram and said, "I am God Almighty, walk before me blameless. I will confirm my covenant between me and you and will greatly increase your numbers." Abram fell facedown, and God said to him, "As for me this is my covenant with you: You will be the father of many nations. No longer will your name be Abram; your name will be Abraham, for I have made you a father of many nations." God's new vision and identity plan begin to unfolded when Abram started to see himself as Abraham. Three months after his name change, Sarah his ninety year old wife, conceived his son Isaac.

Be encouraged today, in Christ we are descendants of Abraham and heirs according to the promise. God has promised us a great future but we must do our part. When we speak by faith as Abraham did, we speak words that agree with what God said. Speaking God's word is speaking from our spirit instead of our head. Our job is to:

hear what God said; speak what God said; see ourselves as God sees us; believe His Word and His plans and then we will receive all that He has promised.

From the Coach:

You will never rise above until you rise above the opinion of others.

Ask Yourself:

What is hindering me from living my purpose and the true identity of who God created me to be?

Follow Peace

Dear Coach,
I need to make a major decision and I am afraid I will make the wrong one. How can I know what to do? – Feeling Alone

Dear Feeling Alone,
We all have experienced times of challenge or uncertainty. People everywhere face major life decisions and as a result many suffer with anxiety, stress or sleeplessness. Some are convinced they can handle everything. They go through life so fast and often miss God. The truth is life can be a collision wreck without direction from God. It's like driving our car 100mph through a red light. Sooner or later someone's going to get hurt. But God loves you and He wants to help you. Right now, no matter where you are or what you may be facing, you are not alone. God knows your name, He knows your every thought, He hears you when you call and He wants to lead you into a place of peace by His Spirit. A place of clarity and direction, a place of refreshing where every burden is removed and every yoke destroyed and where your faith is reactivated.

In John 14:26-27 Jesus promised not to leave us without help. Jesus said, "But the Comforter, Counselor, Helper, Intercessor, Advocate, Strengthener, Standby, the Holy Spirit, Whom the Father will send in My name, in My place, to represent me and act on My behalf, He will teach you all things. And He will cause you to recall (will remind you of, bring to your remembrance) everything I have told you. Peace I leave with you; My own peace I now give you and bequeath to you. Do not let your hearts be troubled, neither let them be afraid. Jesus goes on to say, in the Amplified Bible, "Stop allowing yourself to be agitated and disturbed; and do not permit yourself to be fearful and intimidated and cowardly and unsettled."

The Holy Spirit is your internal navigation system. He is your Comforter, your Counselor. When you spend time in the presence of God, in His word and in prayer, He will direct your path. He knows what you are going through and He knows what is best.

The journey God has for you is exceeding above and beyond all you could ask or think. It is your wealthy place, the reason why you were created. But you must follow peace.

God has specific direction for you. God's plans, pursuits and purposes will get you to the destination He has for you. Be encouraged today, simply pursue peace and you will be pursuing God.

From the Coach:

When making a decision… don't just think about it… think it all the way through. And at the end choose the path that gives you the most peace.

Ask Yourself:

How do I make decisions?

Am I lead by fear or do I slow down and seek God?

> That at the name of Jesus every knee should bow, of those in heaven, and those on earth and of those under the earth, and that every tongue should confess that Jesus Christ is LORD, to the glory of God the Father. – Philippians 2:10-11

The Name of Jesus

Dear Coach,
What's in a name? – Curious

Dear Curious,
In Matthew 1:21, an angel of the Lord appeared to Joseph in a dream and said, "She will give birth to a son, and you are to give him the name Jesus, because he will save his people from their sins."

Have you ever wondered about the importance of a name? As babies we are given a name, often our name has special meaning or family heritage. But when we call upon the name of Jesus and confess Him as Lord, we are adopted into God's family. As members of His family we have access to use the family name and all it represents. In His name there is forgiveness of sins, abundant life, authority, provision, peace, joy, healing, deliverance and everything good.

The name of Jesus is more powerful than any army assembled in the world. And as Christians we have the right to use His name against any attack from the enemy. In Matthew 28:18-20, Jesus tells us that, "All authority in heaven and on earth has been given to me. Therefore go and make disciples of all nations, baptizing them in the name of the Father and of the Son and of the Holy Spirit, and teaching them to obey everything I have commanded you. And surely I am with you always, to the very end of the age."

Then before Jesus ascended to heaven He said in Mark 16:15-18, "Go into all the world and preach the good news to all creation. Whoever believes and is baptized will be saved, but whoever does not believe will be condemned. And these signs will accompany those who believe: **In My name** they will drive out demons; they will speak in new tongues; they will pick up snakes with their hands; and when they drink deadly poison, it will not hurt them at all; they will place their hands on sick people, and they will get well."

God has exalted Jesus to the highest place and gave Him the name that is above every name. At the name of Jesus every knee will bow in heaven, on earth and under the earth and every tongue confess that Jesus is Lord.

Jesus, Jesus, Jesus! Speak the name of Jesus and believe in the power of His name. When you do things change, the miraculous happens and you experience freedom. Be encouraged today, when you speak His name expect to win.

From the Coach:

There is tremendous power in the Name of Jesus.

Ask Yourself:

How am I using the Name of Jesus?

> But those who wait on the Lord shall renew their strength;
> they shall mount up with wings like eagles, They shall run and
> not be weary, They shall walk and not faint. – Isaiah 40:31

Growth Develops Patience

Dear Coach,

I am having a tough time remaining calm, I feel overwhelmed. How can I get control over my emotions? – Keeping it Real

Dear Keeping it Real,

Most of us experience intense times of focus, filled schedules and approaching deadlines. But how can we get it all done, maintain a positive attitude and walk in love? As we grow up spiritually we develop the ability to demonstrate the character of God no matter what is happening around us.

Our everyday activities and interaction with other people deplete our physical and spiritual energy. In fact every non-spiritual activity is burning up spiritual fuel. The secret to a loving and patient lifestyle can be found here in Jude. Jude 1:20 tells us, "But you, beloved, build yourself up founded on your most holy faith, make progress, rise like an edifice (structure) higher and higher, praying in the Holy Spirit; Guard and keep yourself in the love of God; expecting and patiently waiting for the mercy of our Lord Jesus Christ, the Messiah which will bring you into eternal life." He said to guard and keep ourselves in the Love of God.

The love and character of God is defined in 1 Corinthians 13:4-8, "Love endures long and is patient and kind; love never is envious nor boils over with jealousy, is not boastful or vainglorious, does not display itself haughtily. It is not conceited (arrogant and inflated with pride); it is not rude (unmannerly) and does not act unbecomingly. Love (God's love in us) does not insist on its own rights or its own way, for it is not self-seeking; it is not touchy or fretful or resentful; it takes no account of the evil done to it [it pays no attention to a suffered wrong]. It does not rejoice at injustice and unrighteousness, but rejoices when right and truth prevail. Love bears up under anything and everything that comes, is ever ready to believe the best of every person, its hopes are fadeless under all circumstances, and it endures everything [without weakening]. Love never fails [never fades out or becomes obsolete or comes to an end]."

Here love's character is described as patient. Patience is steadfast despite opposition, difficulty or adversity. People often think patience is something you just have but rather it is a decision you make.

Be encouraged today, walking in the Love of God or Agape Love and being patient is a decision to be obedient to God, not a feeling or natural immediate responds. Many times growing up means we have to hold our tongue until our spirit overrides our flesh. Proverbs 15:1 says, "A soft answer turns away wrath, but grievous words stir up anger." It takes patience to restrain our flesh. Our flesh wants to sir it up, pick a fight, throw a tantrum and have everything our way. But God's ways are higher than our ways. God's love has been poured out in our hearts by His Holy Spirit. That outpouring produces the fruit of the Spirit and the character of God. People are not perfect but God's love is, and growth in Him develops patience.

From the Coach:

Growth without change is impossible. Getting stuck in the way it's always been done is more dangerous than the risk of trying the new way.

Ask Yourself:

How do I rest and recharge?

Can I tell when I lose my patience?

Death and life are in the power of the tongue, And those
who love it will eat its fruit. – Proverbs 18:21

Speak Life

Dear Coach,
How can I make change happen in my life? – Same Old, Same Old

Dear Same Old,
The first strategy to creating change is to evaluate what you are
saying. Speaking comes to most people as naturally as breathing. Yet,
on many occasions the words are uttered without conscious thought.
Thousands of words are poured out daily with no understanding of
their creative power. Proverbs 18:21 says, "Death and life are in the
power of the tongue."

Everything we say produces an effect in our world. We are constantly
creating our future either positive or negative with our words. The
area of neurology agrees. Medical science has researched the results
of the spoken word and found that the speech center in the human
brain actually has tremendous control over the body's nervous system.
For example, if someone says, "I am tired." The body then receives
the instructions and prepares to be tried. If someone says, "I am not
qualified to get that promotion." Then right away the body begins to
declare the same thing and behaves accordingly.

Some people have adapted easily to speaking in a negative way. They
are living in the words of the past. They are deceived and believe that
this is as good as it gets. Many even find a false sense of comfort in

using pitiful words to describe their situation and convince others to agree. But in reality they are only making matters worse and prolonging the misery.

If you are going through a challenge in your life, more than ever watch your words. Stop using words to describe your situation and start using words to change your situation. Romans 4:17 says, "the God who gives life to the dead and calls things that are not as though they were." You may not feel blessed, but God said, "You are blessed". You may not feel like confessing by faith what you can't see or understand with your natural mind. You may even wonder how things are ever going to turn around. You must know that God's ways are higher than our ways. When you speak His Word instead of what you see or feel, He is watching over His Word to perform it. Know that right now, God is making a way where there looks like none. The Bible says, "Let the weak say I am strong." Our faith comes by hearing. The more we say something the more we believe it to be true. God's Word is truth. It is time to speak life. It is time to find out and believe what God said over any other source.

God said, "In Jesus Christ, I am saved. I am a new creature. I am a child of the Most High. I am a joint heir with Christ. I am healed, protected and redeemed from the curse of spiritual death, poverty and sickness. I am provided for, delivered, free, loved, and eternally alive. I am strong in the Lord and the power of His might. I am blessed and highly favored. I am an over-comer. I am courageous. I am more than a conquer. I am confident, cleansed, forgiven and bold. I am in the one who has overcome the world. Greater is He that is in me than he who is in the world. No weapon formed against me will ever prosper. God supplies all my needs."

Examine the kinds of things that flow from your mouth. Are you speaking life and blessing? Be encouraged today, God has equipped you with the power to bless your future as you speak His Word over your life everyday.

From the Coach:

A good man brings good things out, and an evil man brings out evil stored up in his heart. For the mouth speaks what the heart is full of. – Luke 6:45

Ask Yourself:

My words are shaping my world, is what I have been saying inline with what I want to see?

If you were of this world, the world would love you as its own;
but because you are not of this world, but I chose you out of
the world, therefore the world hates you. – John 15:19

Love Changes Things

Dear Coach,
I just want to fit in… - Living in this World

Dear Living in this World,
It is natural to want to fit in, to be accepted and adapt to the environment. But as followers of Christ we have been set apart, born again and made a new creation. We are changed from the inside. Our values, speech, actions and life-styles are a reflection of God. Many times true believers don't blend in very well. They clash with and confront the world's darkness, beliefs and systems.

The early Christians of Corinth were struggling with their worldly environment. Corinth was a major cosmopolitan city, a seaport and trade center. It was also filled with idolatry and immorality. Surrounded by corruption and sin the Christians felt pressure to adapt or lower their standards. Their faith was being tried and some of them were failing the test. Paul heard of their struggles, addressed their challenges as well as instructed them in the need for corrective action and clear commitment to Jesus. In 1 Corinthians, Paul calls all of us Christians to be careful not to blend in with the world and accept its values but to live Christ-centered, blameless, loving lives that make a difference for God. That call was to love people where they are but not to take part of their sinfulness.

The Word of God says, "It is the goodness of God that leads a person to repentance." Love not judgment changes things. Paul explains in 1 Corinthians 13:1-13 that love makes our actions and gifts useful. He said, "Without love, I am nothing." As Christians we often examine the actions of other people and offer instruction on how to live a godly life. When we suggest or correct without love we are as Paul says a resounding gong or a clanging cymbal. If we judge people then we become an irritant rather than a positive influence. 1 Corinthians 13:7 says, Love bears up under anything and everything that comes, is ever ready to believe the best of every person, its hopes are fadeless under all circumstances and it endures everything without weakening. This kind of love says, "I believe in you."

Be encouraged today, we are called to believe the best of people, to be salt and light, to walk in the Love of God toward people. We are called to be patient with the world but not like the world. God's ways are higher than our ways. God's love has been poured out in our hearts by His Holy Spirit. That outpouring produces the fruit of the Spirit and the character of God. People are not perfect but God's love is, and His love changes things.

From the Coach:

It is love not judgment that is the catalyst for change.

Ask Yourself:

How can I be more intentional about loving people?

He who does not love does not know God,
for GOD is LOVE. – 1 John 4:8

Do You Know Him?

Dear Coach,
What's the Best question you have ever answered? – In Search of Truth

Dear In Search of Truth,
The greatest question I have ever answered is "Do You Know Him?" God is the creator of all things including all answers and all wisdom. Only in discovering who He is can we truly live.

We live in an instant society with masses of information at our finger tips. With access to the internet or satellite technology we can get the latest breaking news all over the globe. We can know if it's raining in Zimbabwe or who won this year's reality TV challenge; who said what on Capital Hill or who is seeing who in Hollywood. We are a people in the know. My question today is, "Do you know God?

1 John 4:7 says, "Dear friends, let us love one another, for love comes from God. Everyone who loves has been born of God and knows God." When we know God we discover, God is love. And by knowing God our lives will reflect His love to other people. Jesus instructs us in John 13:34, "A new command I give you; Love one another. As I have loved you, so you must love one another. By this all men will know you are my disciples, if you love one another."

Jesus commanded us to love others as He has loved us. Often we are so busy with our own agendas that we get frustrated by interruptions or needs of other people. Not only are we an information society but we are busy people with schedules, meetings, plans and our lists of things to do. There are people all over the world and even in the body of Christ so desperate for God to meet their needs, yet so unwilling to love their neighbor. In 1 John 4 verse 8 John explains that when we don't love, we don't know God, because God is love. When we look into the ministry of Jesus, most of the miracles He preformed took place while He was on His way somewhere else. Jesus took the time, welcomed divine interruptions as He loved people. Jesus was a man on a mission. He was a man of vision and purpose. He was focused yet always took time to meet the needs of those around Him while maintaining a serving and willing attitude. Loving people was a top priority on Jesus' list.

The principles of God work by the ways of God. 1 John 4:16-21 says, "And so we know and rely on the love God has for us. God is love. Whoever lives in love lives in God, and God in him. In this way, love is made complete among us so that we will have confidence on the Day of Judgment, because in this world we are like him. There is no fear in love. But perfect love drives out fear, because fear has to do with punishment. The one who fears is not made perfect in love. We love because he first loved us. If anyone says, "I love God," yet hates his brother, he is a liar. For anyone who does not love his brother, whom he has seen, cannot love God, whom he has not seen. And he has given us this command: Whoever loves God must also love his brother."

Be encouraged today, when you receive Jesus as Lord and Savior, His perfect love comes to live in your heart. He lived to show the example of how we can have the abundant life He promised. As you spend time with Him, His love will transform you and cause you to love those around you. Every promise from God works by love Put loving others on your" To Do" list today and see God do a mighty work in your life.

Tammy Holyfield

Getting to know God's character and learning to trust Him will change everything.

Ask Yourself:

How well do I know the character of God?

Bonus: Some of My Favorite Quotes

One of the essentials to success is doing what needs to be done regardless of how you feel.

A bad attitude is like a flat tire, you won't get anywhere until you change it!

You don't have to chase what belongs to you.

Only thinking about today will steal your future. Successful people delay gratification while working on the life of their dreams.

Growth without change is impossible. Getting stuck in the way it's always been done is more dangerous than the risk of trying the new way.

Money is ultimately never enough compensation for doing a job. Find something that blends your skills, abilities, personality traits, values, dreams, and passion. When you do, you will be unstoppable!!!

You can't please God by focusing on your own natural abilities. Trust Him to do what you can't.

Pray like it all depends on God while you work like it all depends on you.

Your beliefs don't make you a better person... Your BEHAVIOR does!

Going through a challenge does NOT make you an inadequate person. It's easy to feel embarrassed or ashamed about circumstances. Winners allow those "feelings" to inspire creative innovations to not only change their environment but unlock potential in others.

You know it's time for the next phase of action when the urgency of the vision consumes your thinking.

Whatever you think of the most is what you will get more of. Success begins with training your brain to focus on positive, profitable solutions.

The measure of a truly great person is the level of courtesy and respect with which they treat someone who can do nothing for them!

"You will become as small as your controlling desire or as great as your dominant aspiration." - James Allen

"Success requires 2 things, knowing exactly what you want and determining the price you are willing to pay." H. L. Hunt

"Believe in yourself and there will come a day when others will have no choice but to believe with you." C. Kersey

"You were born to WIN; but to be a winner you must plan to win, prepare to win and expect to win!" Zig Ziglar

"You can buy fun but don't chase happiness with money... you will never catch it!"...Dave Ramsey

"Faith is my grip on God! Grace is God's grip on me!

"Life is better lived by design than by default." – Steven Covey

A goal without a plan is just a wish.

A piggy bank with two nickels makes a whole lot more noise than a fill one! Beware of broke people trying to criticize your dreams and talk you out of your own success.

The busier you are the more critical it is to plan. Planning produces PEACE!

I will go before you and I will level the mountains. I will break down gates of bronze and cut through bars of iron. I will give you hidden treasures, riches stored in hidden places, so that you know that I am the LORD, the God of Israel, who summons you by name. - Isaiah 45:2-3

"In Today's economy, intelligence is a form of property. Focused intelligence, the ability to acquire and apply knowledge is the new source of wealth." Peter Drucker

It's not what is being said about you but what you believe about you that you become.

Today may not be "The End of the World" but we should live like everyday might be. LIVE READY! #prioritize

Destiny doesn't have a plan B.

Holiness will stimulate the US economy.

People don't follow titles they follow courage and integrity.

You cannot manage time only yourself within it.

How do you respond to the storm? Who you are proceeds what you do... Leadership begins with the heart. People before processes.

Great LEADERS create opportunities for their people to operate in their gifts and talents. What happens to the team when members constantly play "out of position"? It's like having the QB play right tackle... Someone is going to get HURT. Are your people in the right place in your organization?

Just like a diamond... it's the pressure and heat that demands me to change.

Fashion Tip for Today... Wearing a bad attitude makes you look fat.

What you are attentive to grows... What you ignore dies.

Discipline is the bridge between goals and results.

When you are disappointed by what you don't have it steals from what you already have. Dream BIG while being grateful.

You get the best efforts from others not by LIGHTING a fire beneath them, but by BUILDING a fire within.

When pursuing goals, its not what you get but who you become that gives life meaning.

What you sow, you will grow.

Only you can decide if you will become all you were created to be or settle for where you are.

My choices establish habits good or bad. I am a product of my choices not of the circumstances surrounding me. I have the freedom to choose my responses based on principles and not on outside influences.

Success is relevant to where you started not how long it took to get there!

www.TammyHolyfield.com

LEADERSHIP: You can buy a person's hand but never their heart. There are 4 dimensions of human motivation. As leaders we must understand what attracts people to be part of our team and how to keep them engaged. These dimensions are based on human needs so as each level is met we advance to the next level.

The difference between a dream and a goal is a PLAN!" Dream Big...Plan Now! All things are possible for those who believe! What are your Biggest Dreams?

Great leaders have the capacity to see future potential.

High performance achievement is not based on wondering.... It's based on purpose!

The only way to stay the course is to stay close to the One who predestined it.

"The recession won't be over till we raise a generation that knows how to live on what they've got." - Dave Ramsey

Fear sees what man sees; Faith sees what God sees. Fear creates paralysis while Faith creates action.

Bonus:

Journey Navigation®
Charting the Course from Where YOU Are to Where YOU Want
to Be!

What is Journey Navigation®?

Journey Navigation® is a life-changing program that teaches
you to live a more purposeful life while achieving your highest
priorities, goals and dreams. During this exciting process you
can expect to discover and implement effective habits of increased
focus, communication, personal planning, personal and business
growth, eliminating debt, saving for the future, and giving like
never before. You will be challenged and motivated to plan for
your life, your money and change your future forever.

Journey Navigation® (JN) consists of a 13-week success process
curriculum—taught by leadership expert Tammy Holyfield —
that incorporates proven, practical Fortune 500 business strategic
planning principles with small-group discussions to encourage
accountability and discipleship. Journey Navigation® is highly
interactive, radically energetic and entertaining for everyone, with
a unique combination of humor, thought provoking activities,
informative advice and biblical messages. Many businesses,
ministries and individuals have already had their lives changed
by attending Journey Navigation.

Journey Navigation® Self ~ Evaluation

Name: _____ Date: _____

Please rate the following 1 to 10 with 10 being perfect. Using complete honesty, circle the number that indicates how you are presently performing.

<u>Personal Leadership</u>
1. Consistent in Daily Bible Reading, Prayer and Spiritual Growth
        1 2 3 4 5 6 7 8 9 10
2. Demonstrates strong faith and Godly character
        1 2 3 4 5 6 7 8 9 10
3. Has a firm grasp of Biblical principles
        1 2 3 4 5 6 7 8 9 10
4. Maintains self control and leads well in public
        1 2 3 4 5 6 7 8 9 10
5. Represents the Christian faith with excellence in public places
        1 2 3 4 5 6 7 8 9 10
6. Arrives early or on time
        1 2 3 4 5 6 7 8 9 10
7. Demonstrates excellence in managing time, schedules and tasks.
        1 2 3 4 5 6 7 8 9 10
8. Honors commitments and keeps promises.
        1 2 3 4 5 6 7 8 9 10

<u>Leading Others</u>
1. Communicates expectations with clarity
        1 2 3 4 5 6 7 8 9 10
2. Leads with the spirit of grace, honor and respect for others
        1 2 3 4 5 6 7 8 9 10
3. Is optimistic; takes the attitude that most problems can be solved
        1 2 3 4 5 6 7 8 9 10
4. Develops people by coaching, teaching, training and mentoring
        1 2 3 4 5 6 7 8 9 10

5. Sees the need to cross train and actively duplicate functions
   1 2 3 4 5 6 7 8 9 10
6. Models servant leadership and is not self promoting
   1 2 3 4 5 6 7 8 9 10

Outstanding Teamwork

1. Understands the perspective that God created each of us with different strengths
   1 2 3 4 5 6 7 8 9 10
2. Seeks common ground in an effort to resolve conflicts and maintain unity
   1 2 3 4 5 6 7 8 9 10
=3. Works harmoniously with other people
   1 2 3 4 5 6 7 8 9 10
4. Identifies and removes barriers to effective teamwork
   1 2 3 4 5 6 7 8 9 10

Journey Navigation® Self ~ Evaluation Page 2

5. Maintains smooth, effective working relationships
   1 2 3 4 5 6 7 8 9 10
6. Shows a willingness to listen and be open to input
   1 2 3 4 5 6 7 8 9 10
7. Encourages feedback and ideas from other people
   1 2 3 4 5 6 7 8 9 10

Execution of Goals and Objectives

1. Ensures clear accountability for important task or objectives
   1 2 3 4 5 6 7 8 9 10
2. Keeps promises and honor commitments
   1 2 3 4 5 6 7 8 9 10
3. Acts with a sense of urgency
   1 2 3 4 5 6 7 8 9 10
4. Rallies support to get things done
   1 2 3 4 5 6 7 8 9 10

Outstanding Service
1. Interacts with people in a kind and professional manner
     1 2 3 4 5 6 7 8 9 10
2. Builds strong relationships
     1 2 3 4 5 6 7 8 9 10
3. Listens carefully to peoples' needs
     1 2 3 4 5 6 7 8 9 10
4. Takes action to meet peoples' needs and concerns
     1 2 3 4 5 6 7 8 9 10
5. Succeeds in viewing a situation through others' eyes
     1 2 3 4 5 6 7 8 9 10
6. Is moved with compassion for people
     1 2 3 4 5 6 7 8 9 10

Accountability
1. Prevents unpleasant surprises by communicating important information
     1 2 3 4 5 6 7 8 9 10
2. Confronts conflicts promptly so it does not escalate
     1 2 3 4 5 6 7 8 9 10
3. Takes responsibility for his/her actions without blaming others
     1 2 3 4 5 6 7 8 9 10
4. Understands what motivates other people to perform at their best
     1 2 3 4 5 6 7 8 9 10
5. Accountable to a spouse, leader or Pastor
     1 2 3 4 5 6 7 8 9 10
5. Willing to listen and adjust when corrected
     1 2 3 4 5 6 7 8 9 10